HONEY, WHY ARE WE POOR?

Steve Harris

Printed in the Federal Republic of Nigeria by:
Enbelo Company Limited.
08170000167.
design@enbelo.com
www.enbelo.com

First Printing, 2019

ISBN 978-978-976-586-7

Cover design by: Akinlabi Akinbulumo @mrphisha
Editors: Chisom Ojukwu, @wordsarework
Publishers: The Steve Harris Company

OUTLINE

DEDICATION

To Imma

No one really knows how useless I am without you; but they do now. Thank you for helping me birth this book. Thank you for reading every version, for every comment and suggestion and most importantly, never letting me quit. This is your book.

To Paryss

My ceiling, no matter how great, will be your floor.

Daddy loves you.

ENDORSEMENTS

Act on it and thank Steve Harris when your purse begins to fatten

Honey, Why Are We Poor addresses the less obvious financial behaviors that may be causing financial stress in your life! It chronicles the journey of a couple as they learn the simple things they can begin to do to get out of the rat race and become rich.

Steve Harris delivers this book in a simple and humorous language that not only makes it easy to read but is also a a must have in your library if you really want to be rich. Anyone can relate to the characters in the book, whether young or old, single or marred, man or woman, as long as you are serious about becoming financially free. But don't just add it to your library, ACT ON IT and thank Steve Harris when you purse begins to fatten!

Tolu Dima-Okojie
Money Behaviour Strategist

Honey, Why Are We Poor mixes Steve Harris' frank talking, witty and engaging personality with practical life lessons that is definitely a must read!

If you need a book that breaks down sound financial principles in an easy to digest manner, look no further.

Honey, Why Are We Poor, mixes Steve Harris' frank talking, witty and engaging personality with practical life lessons that is definitely a must read!

Peace Hyde
Head Digital Media and Partnerships/ WA Correspondent, Forbes Africa.

This book was certainly worth the wait

Just by reading this book, I can tell it was not an easy one to write. A lot of work must have gone into making it fun, relatable and simple enough without losing the essence and purpose for which it was created.

This book will make you think, remember, reconsider and hopefully, redesign your financial situation whatever it currently is.

It is presented in a way that will make you laugh at your ignorance but still feel hopeful about the future, I daresay some people might experience shock when they find themselves vividly described in the pages of this book.

I received the first draft of this book in July 2015 and knowing Steve Harris to be a ruthless executor, I never really understood why it took so long to finish his 3rd book.

But when he told me that he had to live the process first, test, fail and come up with a proven systematic approach to dealing with money issues so he was better positioned to help others, I grew a newfound respect for him (and I already love & respect him very much by the way).

In an age where people just want to slam their names on book covers so they can be called an author with little or no value placed on the content of the book and the impact on its readers, it says a lot about a persons character that Steve would commit himself for years, not break under society's pressure to produce anything for the sake of it, but follow his heart to publish such a beautiful piece that truly helps people.

I know that this book will get into many hands, touch many lives, turn around the finances of many and the ripple effect will not be contained.

This book was certainly worth the wait.

Remi Owadokun
4 Time Amazon Best Selling Author & Founder, Total Makeover Program

I wish I had this gift 8 years ago when I started my corporate career.

This is the first time I read a book that made me feel like the writer understood me and created a practical solution to change my life for good.

Honey, Why Are We Poor will reduce the number of corporate employees as well as entrepreneurs that are indeed poor as well as spur more people to dare to dream.

I strongly recommend this book to every African employee & entrepreneur, especially if you have ever asked yourself; is this the best my life can be?

Then read this book. Apply the strategies and watch your life move from an employee enduring your job to an employee empowered enough to rise higher than your present circumstances.

Thank you Steve for blessing this generation with a gift I wish I had 8 years ago when I started my corporate career.

God bless you abundantly.

Just Ibe
Sales Expert & CEO Just Ibe Consulting

Steve Harris has taken the lessons I've learned understanding money over the last 20 years and made them so simple, a four year old could understand them.

I have spent the last 2 decades of my life, on a quest to understand how money works, and create sustainable wealth. In that time I have had to attend multiple seminars and read different books on the subject, some at least 5 times, to understand the principles expounded therein.

Steve Harris has taken the lessons of the last 20 years and made them stupidly simple, a four year old could understand them. He has done so with humor while passing across a message of Personal Responsibility.

'Honey, why are we poor?' is a book every and anyone, who desires to build sustainable wealth must read. It provides the reader, with the tools to wrestle back control of their finances and by extension, their lives!

I wouldn't hesitate to recommend this book to anyone seeking to exit the rat race and attain financial mastery.

Edwin West
Financial Expert & Wealth Coach

Steve, I will be mad at you if you don't have Total Money Workout events for working professionals and mini sessions to improve their finances and help them explore investment opportunities.

This is the kind of book that knocks you off your socks instantly. I found myself literally asking questions about my financial fitness, reaffirming my empire and looking for budgeting apps here and there.

Again this book jolts you into action and makes you want to be better, not just for yourself, but for generations after you.

Steve, I will be mad at you if you don't have Total Money Workout events for working professionals and mini sessions to improve their finances and help them explore investment opportunities.

Thank you for not being selfish with your knowledge and journey and for making it ever more relatable, simple and straight to the point.

There are so many Soma's and Ezzy's out there but very few Toks' and Tolu's.

Guys you cannot afford not to buy this book, it is critical at this stage I can attest.

Thanks, Steve Harris for this.

Nnanke Essien
International Speaker & Business Improvement Manager

You cannot read this book, apply the recommended principles and remain poor

Honey, Why Are We Poor is such a beautifully written book by Steve Harris. From the minute I started reading, I could not stop; it makes such a captivating read. I particularly love the switches in scenes; I felt like I was watching a movie.

I was also intrigued with the way Steve creatively and subtly infused his learning points on the laws of wealth.

Frankly, you cannot read this book, apply the recommended principles and remain poor. No! Never!

This book is loaded with wisdom for creating and sustaining abundance and I greatly recommend it.

Enjoy this masterpiece and thank me later. Bravo Steve! Bravo!!!

Bankole Williams
Founder, Live Your Dreams Africa

PREFACE

THURSDAY
VERITAS AD AGENCY, LEKKI
4:47pm

Meet Ezekiel.

Age 44, 5'11, 237 pounds, married 8 years, 2 kids, a pet pooch called Scruffy and enjoys the good life.

'Ezzy' as his friends call him, is a marketing consultant with one of the top advertising agencies in the country. Slowly, but surely, he's climbing the ladder of success, one rung at a time, and fancies himself sitting in the C.E.O's chair someday (but that's our little secret).

Ezzy's doing pretty well for himself, drives a Honda Accord 2006 model, fondly referred to as the "End of Discussion", earns N4.2 million annually and lives in a comfortable 3-bedroom apartment in Surulere.

"Man, thank God, the work day's over," Ezzy remarked to his pal, Deji.

"Yeah, I thought it'd never end," said Deji. "We better head to The Lounge to cool off before we get stuck in some major traffic."

"Right behind you," Ezzy concurred, "let me get my jacket. Mind you, you're buying."

"Don't count on it!" Deji replied.

Ezzy laughed. It had been a good day, and the evening looked like it would get better.

I wonder what Soma's up to, he thought.

GULF CAPITAL, LEKKI
LADIES' ROOM
5:48pm

"Somaaaa! Are you in there?" called Amaka.

"You can't hide forever. The B.M.'s been ringing your desk for the last 5 minutes for the report and he's put a bounty on your head. He wants you dead or alive, now the whole bank's looking for you."

"How much am I worth?" Soma asked.

"3K. And I'm here to collect."

"Tell him you didn't find me and I'll give you two hundred naira."

"You're not serious. Make it five hundred and I'll swear we never had this conversation."

"Oooh, Amaka, you know that if I see the B.M now, I won't leave here on time; I might as well kiss my evening goodbye."

"I'll give you 5 minutes to escape or else, you're toast," Amaka joked.

"Thanks love, you're the best," Soma cheered. 5:57pm, she thought. 3 minutes to go.

Meet Soma.

Age 37, 5'5, 168 pounds (optimal weight, 125 pounds), 3-time 'Miss Campus Hotlegs' (2004 – 2007) of the University of Ibadan – a feat she's extremely proud of and legs she's still proud to show off, mother of Ezzy's 2 kids, a banker with Gulf Capital, one of Nigeria's leading financial institutions and presently hiding in the ladies' room.

Soma's doing pretty well for herself. She's risen from youth corps member to the rank of a Banking Officer (BO) in 7 years and the sky seems to be her starting point.

As Soma navigated through the Island's traffic, she thought about how fortunate and blessed she was.

She snuggled deeper into the leather seat of her Toyota Corolla which she was almost done paying for – the bank had financed her car loan and was steadily debiting her salary account with N50,000 monthly.

"I'll be glad when it's over," Soma soliloquized as she hummed to Burna Boy's hit track, Killin' Dem over her CD player.

With her good job, she was the envy of many of her friends. Pay could be better, she thought. But she hadn't done too badly.

Can't wait to get home. These shoes are killing me.

HOME
8:43pm

"Hey, honey, how was work?" Ezzy asked as Soma trudged into their living room and slumped, exhausted, into the large leather sofa.

"Don't ask. Where do I even begin?" Soma replied lazily as she began to recall the events of her well-worn day.

"Well, thank God it's over," Ezzy said, running his fingers through her tousled hair.

"Uh huh." Soma hurried into the children's bedroom. They're asleep. Oh no, not again! She realized that for the third consecutive time that week, she had lost the opportunity to tuck her children into bed.

Damn this job, she swore for the umpteenth time. There's got to be a better way.

"Honey, don't forget that it's Dave and Amara's wedding next weekend, and you promised you'd give me some money for the aso-ebi," Soma said.

"Yeah, whatever," Ezzy muttered under his breath.

"Also, the children's school fees are due by Friday. You promised to take care of it," she continued, oblivious of Ezzy's increased discomfort. "I also noticed some funny noises coming from my car. Could you please ask the mechanic to come over? I think it's due for a tune-up."

"Whoa, Soma, give me a break!" Ezzy yelled. "You haven't been home 30 minutes and you've started nagging about bills. Aso-ebi today, DSTV tomorrow, don't you ever stop?"

"Ezekiel, don't raise your voice at me, the children are asleep," Soma hissed.

"I'm sorry, but I feel so choked by all these bills. It seems we have more bills than money," her husband moaned.

Stunned for the moment, Soma looked around their living room. It was well furnished with the silent, 'split unit' air conditioning system, plush leather seats, dimmed light fittings, Persian rugs, parquet floors, a High Definition Smart Television and the latest Home Theatre System. She took it all in, sighed deeply and with tears streaming down her face, she turned back to Ezzy and asked:

"Honey, why are we poor?"

BEFORE YOU TAKE THIS BOOK HOME WITH YOU...

Does this scene seem familiar?

You'd be surprised to discover that it plays itself out in most homes rather frequently.

It may even be playing out in your home right now.

Now, while I don't subscribe to the theory of evolution – man being a direct descendant of chimpanzees and monkeys doesn't quite sit well with me – I do believe that poverty has also undergone evolution.

Poverty has evolved from the street beggar asking for alms and the street kids forcibly washing your windshield and demanding payment, to a more sophisticatedoutlook.

Today, poverty isn't only found on the sidewalk, but it's also found in corporations and boardrooms. It has a job, wears a nice suit and expensive clothes, drives a nice car, lives in a nice part of town AND IS BROKE!

I hope you picked up this book (and bought it, or at least intend to) not only because it had a really catchy title, but because somewhere, deep inside, you desire to learn, understand and experience true wealth.

There are a lot of books written about money or wealth that promise you a get-rich-quick answer or an 'instant solution'.

THIS IS NOT ONE OF THEM.

It took me 7 years to write this book because I had to live it. I experienced many of the highs and lows you'll connect to in this book. So I'm not sharing my knowledge from theory or some book I read, I've been there, done that, bought the t-shirt and I've got all the scars to prove it and better still, I'm financially free and that's what I'm trying to do for you.

This book is not intended to be an ornament or an addition to your well-stocked library either; it's a manual for you to get productive and DO SOMETHING!

If you aren't going to do something with it, may I politely advise that you put it back on the shelf and move on to the next interesting title that catches your fancy?

But if you're interested in getting out of the 'rat race', living a fulfilled life and walking into the rest of the best years of your life, this is the book for you.

So what are you waiting for? Take the book to the counter, pay for it and let's get moving!

We have a lot of work to do.

It's time for a total money workout!

CHAPTER ONE

WHO'S THE BOSS?

Secret 1: Money makes a wonderful servant, but a terrible master! - *Francis Bacon*

FRIDAY
THE LOUNGE
8:48pm

"Dear God, I'm finished!" Ezzy muttered under his breath for the eight time as he sipped his second glass of whiskey. He sat at the bar, waiting for the traffic heading to Lagos Mainland to subside. Soma's words echoed through his mind, reverberating like a tidal wave that could only be dulled with each sip of whiskey.

Honey, why are we poor?

"Poor? What does she mean we're poor?" Ezzy pondered. "See this babe. We have a nice apartment, good jobs, drive nice cars, send the kids to good schools, earn a good living between us and can afford the finer things of life. So what does she mean by saying we're poor?!" He took another sip of his whiskey.

"Didn't expect to see you here," a deep voice boomed behind him, revealing a tall, light-skinned gentleman who pulled up a bar stool and sat beside Ezzy.

"Hey, Toks, it's been a while. I only see you on the news and in tabloids. You don turn celeb," Ezzy thumped the newcomer heartily on the back. "What are you doing here and where've you been hiding?"

"Same as you man, got swamped with work at the office and lost track of time. I wasn't ready for the drive through traffic and so, decided to stop by the Lounge to wait it out," Toks replied.

Ezzy smiled, but deep inside, he envied him. This one-time University of Benin course mate of his seemed to be living a charmed life.

Tokunbo had it all. He had a very successful consulting firm, which always seemed to be facilitating or executing one huge business deal or the other. He was the darling of the media, a respected pillar of the community, nothing ever scandalous was ever mentioned about him. He was always involved in one noteworthy project or the other. He also lived in the best part of town, his marriage was exemplary and his kids were so smart, the epitome of what well-mannered children should be.

"So what brings you here? You seem to have a lot on your mind. What's the matter?" Toks asked.

"Just needed to drown my sorrows a bit and rue my existence," replied Ezzy. "And if you must know, I had a slight disagreement with Soma last night."

"What was it about?"

"What do you think?" Ezzy retorted. "It was about money, cheddar, cheese, moolah, the benjaminsor whatever people call it these days. I mean, would you believe that she had the effrontery to call us poor? How could she say that? We both have great jobs, working our way up the corporate ladder, I mean, we have a few loans to be repaid here and there, but come on, who doesn't?"

Ezzy ended his rant by telling Toks about all what had occurred the night before. When he was done, Toks took a huge breath and sighed deeply.

"I see this all the time," he said to Ezzy.

"See what?" Ezzy asked.

Toks got off his chair and stretched his 6-foot 2-inch frame.

"Ezzy, I've been around the world more times than I can count, I've gone through several ups and downs with my business, I've lost huge sums of money and thrice, I have almost quit on my dreams. One thing I've learned through the bitter swill of personal experience is that you've got to respect the secret of true riches."

"Secret of true riches, huh? You sound like you've found Aladdin's magic lamp,"Ezzy smirked.

"I guess I have," Toks continued, "but I must admit, your wife's right; you are poor."

"What do you mean? Are you insane?" Ezzy growled. "I know you're considered to be quite smart, my dear Toks, but this time I think you're one sandwich short from a picnic basket." Ezzy scoffed.

Toks shrugged. "Whatever man, but let me ask you this. How long would you and your family survive without begging, borrowing or stealing if you lost your job today?"

The profundity of the question hit Ezzy like an anvil as his mind began to conjure different scenarios of loss, termination from his job, foreclosure on his mortgage and a consequent loss of economic status.

"Dear God, I'm finished!" he muttered under his breath.

For the 9th time.

THE LOUNGE
9:03pm

"Soma was right after all, we're poor." Ezzy muttered under his breath. "Why are women always right?!"

He listened intently as Toks shared his first secret.

"Ezzy, money makes a wonderful servant, but a terrible master. Listen to me, man, money's like a woman: you must treat her with respect. If you have a vision that's beyond you and a serious, strategic plan to take you to that destination, she'll stay with you. But if you treat her with disrespect and try to use her, she'll turn the tables on you and dump you like a stale loaf of bread."

Ezzy knew that Toks was right. He actually felt like a stale loaf of bread.

Toks continued, "I don't mean to sound preachy, but quoting from the Bible in Ecclesiastes 10:19, it says: a feast is made for laughter, and wine makes merry; but money answers all things.

"Yeah, I know that one. The latter part's my favourite scripture," Ezzy smiled as he poured another drink.

"It's good to know you flip through your Bible," Toks scoffed. "Anyways, back to my analogy. Now, for money to answer all things, it means it must be submissive; therefore, we can say it's a servant, capisce?"

"Capisce, Godfather," Ezzy mocked, in an imitation of an Italian mobster in 'The Godfather' movie, based on Mario Puzo's novel.

Toks rolled his eyes and sighed. His old friend hadn't changed a bit.

"As I was saying, imagine money as a servant, ready to do your bidding. It often comes at the time of the month you receive your pay check; and when it does, it expects you to have a planned schedule of activities or duties you require it to perform, which is called a budget. If you can provide that budget, money defers to you and becomes your servant; but if you're unable to provide one, money turns the tables on you and automatically becomes your master.

"As you know, money has no leadership capacity, so it leads you along a cycle of ruin of huge shopping sprees and instant gratification choices. But when the scales have fallen off your eyes, you suddenly realize that the cash is gone and you're worse off than when you first got it." Toks explained.

"Man, that's exactly what happens to me every month!" Ezzy exclaimed. "Come to think of it, it also happened last month.

"But wait a sec, Toks, you expect me to believe that the reason I'm broke today is because I don't have a budget?"

"That's one of the reasons. I know it sounds elementary, but think about it. Every door could either be an access or an obstacle. Most doors usually have three components, which could turn what used to be an obstacle into an access point. Any ideas?"

"Yeah, wood, paint and nails," Ezzy laughed hysterically.

"Try harder, wise guy." Toks grinned. "The key, the door handle and the hinges. They're so much smaller than the door, but once activated, turn what originally should be an obstacle into an opportunity. The principle here is that small keys open big doors. The steps to go from poverty to financial freedom are often found in what we don't consider as obvious.

"Listen man, I gotta go. The traffic should have eased off by now. Here's my card, give me a call sometime. Perhaps we can get you off the broad road where many are unfortunately on their way to financial ruin, onto the straight and narrow lane of financial mastery where some of us reside."

And with those words, he walked off.

"Financial ruin, yeah right!" Try as he did, Ezzy couldn't shrug the feeling that Toks was right.

TOTAL MONEY WORKOUT

1. Answer this:

   How long would you and your family survive without begging, borrowing or stealing if you lost your job today?

2. What would happen if you lost your source of livelihood today?
3. Do you have a budget?

CHAPTER TWO

USED AND DUMPED?

Secret 2: Money that is unplanned for comes with the gift of selective amnesia when its use is not documented.

SATURDAY
11.15AM

There's nothing like a good old shopping spree to put a little pep in your step, Soma thought as she wandered down the aisle, perusing several racks for the latest in women's clothing and accessories.

"I'll take this one, and that one, hmm, this looks interesting." She picked up several items of clothing. After all I've been through over the past month, this calls for a celebration.

Soma did have cause to celebrate, as she'd bagged an A+ in her last appraisal and had been recommended for promotion to the position of a Senior Banking Officer.

I deserve a treat to reward myself after jumping through so many hoops for the bank, my husband and the kids. I need some 'me' time.

As Soma walked to the counter to pay for her items, she accidentally bumped into a lady intently examining the prices of several shoes on a rack.

"I'm so sorry," she apologized, as she stepped back to make sure the lady was okay. "Are you hurt?"

"I'm fine, but you really do need to watch where you're-" the lady stopped mid-sentence as she recognized her unwitting assailant. "Soma, is it really you? It's a lie!" she shrieked as she gave Soma a hug.

"Tolu, where've you been?" Soma shrieked as she reciprocated the hug, her smile incredulous.

"Here, there and everywhere," Tolu responded.

It seemed just like yesterday that both ladies were colleagues in the same department of the bank, going about their daily routine until they heard a 'rumour' that the Management Team was considering downsizing due to the harsh realities of the economic crisis, as well as several new reforms that had been introduced by the new Governor of the Central Bank. They had shrugged off the rumours as hearsay until Tolu came to work one Wednesday morning and found out that she couldn't gain access or clearance into her work computer. She tried a couple of times, but her password kept getting denied.

"What the heck? Could someone get me Ahmed from Info Tech? I can't seem to log into my system," she had yelled.

For Tolu, time seemed to have slowed down as the Branch Manager asked her to come into his office; one hasty conversation followed, a piercing scream, Tolu's head bowed with tears streaming down her face as she ran past Soma into the Ladies room.

That day, Tolu had lost her job.

That was 3 years ago. They had promised to keep in touch and be there for each other, but somehow, never did. Now, by sheer coincidence, their paths had crossed.

Soma felt the cold fingers of shame wrap themselves around her. "Tolu, I'm so sorry that I didn't keep in touch; I don't know what to say. I have no excuses." She apologized with eyes fixed to the floor.

"It's okay, don't you worry about it," Tolu shrugged it off graciously.

"Do you have time for a bite to eat? I want to hear what you've been up to."

"That would be great. It'd be just like old times."

"Let's go then." Soma picked up her 'treasure trove' of clothes and led the way; she noted that Tolu hadn't bought anything.

As they sat down to lunch, Tolu began her tale: "Soma, if I had to do it all differently, I would. If I ever had an inkling that I'd lose my job 3 years into my career, I would have made much wiser decisions. Now, with the benefit of hindsight, I live in regret.

"Recently, I was at a seminar on Financial Fitness and I heard a Life Strategist say that 'we only recognize opportunities that we missed yesterday, tomorrow'."

Soma agreed. What opportunities am I missing today? she pondered.

Immediately, her mind went to several of the savings and investment products that the bank had developed, but she had never taken advantage of; rather she had always focused on the consumer loan products.

I'm such a fool, she thought. "Wait first. What's a Life Strategist? Sounds snazzy."

"I know right? Well, he explained what he does by saying that every human being has 7 dimensions to their lives; mental, physical, relationships, business or career, financial, societal and spiritual and each of these dimensions are closely linked, such that if one goes out of balance, it affects the entire dynamic of the individual."

"Makes sense so far," Soma concurred. "I know how out of sorts I feel when I'm broke or I have an argument with my husband, it definitely affects my productivity."

"Exactly!" Tolu replied. "So what the Life Strategist does is to help his clients identify the area that's imbalanced, determine strategy or goals for resolution and then, drives the client to ruthless execution within a specified time period."

"Ruthless execution. I definitely like the sound of that." Soma smiled.

"Yeah, he said a lot of people desire to achieve their goals, but there's a huge execution gap because most people don't know how to determine the right course of action and follow through." Tolu swatted at a fly hovering around her drink.

"He's definitely talking about me," Soma smiled. "I should get me a Life Strategist."

"Don't worry, Soma, I'll hook you up."

"Thanks dear. So what else did he say during the seminar?" Soma asked.

Tolu continued, "he said that we celebrate tomorrow when we seize the right opportunities today".

That's a huge one, Soma reflected quietly. What opportunities have I seized lately?

Here, Soma drew a blank.

"You know, Soma," Tolu continued, "as bankers and career professionals, we fail to realize that we live a life of illusion that gives us a false perception of security."

"How do you mean a life of illusion?" Soma asked.

"Open your eyes, Soma," Tolu sighed.

"Don't you get it? We go to work at high-end establishments with fully air conditioned offices, drive the latest posh cars as the envy of our family and friends; but if truth be told, we know that behind all those posh accessories which our bank accounts constantly get debited for, we go home broke!"

Soma couldn't help but agree. Her recent argument with Ezzy was still freshly ingrained in her subconscious.

"I used to live life from pay check to pay check. Outwardly, I looked like a symbol of success and because I was good at my job, I could afford some of the nice things of life. Soma, you wouldn't believe some of the things I splurged on.

"I mean, I used to buy jewelry from that lady who always seemed to give us great deals by letting us pay in three installments by giving her post-dated cheques. Do you remember her?"

"How could I forget?" Soma replied. "I still owe her fifty thousand naira sef."

"I mean, I was an impulsive buyer," Tolu continued. "I'd buy shoes, clothes, get my hair done at really posh salons, take holiday trips abroad, and even buy things I didn't need – because they looked pretty, or just to prove that I could. I thought I was living the life, but I was wrong. I never gave much thought to planning my finances, drawing up a budget or should I say, sticking to my budget," she laughed.

"That's the hard part." Soma laughed too.

Her friend seemed so much wiser. Wisdom gained from personal experience no doubt.

Tolu continued, "I never felt that I had need of those things. I figured that I'd continue to rise in my career and be able to do more for myself until I was able to resign and start my own company. I was so wrong.

"But you know, when you don't have a plan for money, money makes plans for you. It lures you into a having a false sense of security, believing that the goose that lays the golden eggs will keep on giving, until you wake up one morning to discover that the goose has been cooked."

"That's scary," Soma chipped in.

"So when the bubble burst and I lost my job, I soon discovered that I could no longer maintain the lifestyle that I'd so painstakingly built. All this time, I foolishly believed that I'd kept something away for the rainy day-"

"Did you?" Soma interjected with deep concern.

"I had, but it barely scratched the surface," Tolu replied. "I mean, what use is an umbrella when you're drowning in a flood?"

Soma almost fell off her seat. That word hit too close to home. What use is an umbrella when you're drowning in a flood? Was she drowning? Were her savings and investments an umbrella that she had to carry or a boat that could carry her?

She knew the answer.

"With my finances in the sorry state that they were," Tolu continued, "I felt used by money, and unceremoniously dumped. It felt like High School all over again."

"But what about Ade?" Soma asked, referring to Tolu's then fiancé, now husband of 2 years.

"He tried his best. He's a good man. But with the wedding coming up in a few months, we were already stretched at the seams. The good thing about this whole episode was that we were all the more adamant to refuse our families when they insisted that we have a grand wedding. We knew where the shoe hurt us and so we firmly put our foot down and refused."

"Good for you." Soma thumped her fist on the table.

"Babe, I've realized that after the wedding, marriage begins."

"That's true," agreed Soma.

"My advice to intending married couples these days is to never waste all your hard-earned money on a short three to four-hour ceremony to impress people who don't care about you, know you, love you or have your best interests at heart; because if they did, they would advise you to plan for the marriage, and not just the wedding. If your family wants a big wedding, let them pay for it."

"Gbamatozoa!" Soma thumped the table a second time.

"There are so many stereotypes in our culture that should be eliminated because they cause us so much more harm, than good." Tolu added.

"I agree," Soma said, "but what did you do to make the difference in your finances?"

"Remember that Life Strategist that I talked about earlier?"

"Yeah, what about him?"

"Well, he taught me something so profound," Tolu continued. "That secret has proven to be a game changer in my finances."

"Well, what did he say?" Soma couldn't bear the suspense.

"Relax, I'll tell you. He said that money that is unplanned for comes with the gift of selective amnesia when its use is not documented."

Soma pondered that thought for a moment as Tolu continued quickly.

"Have you ever noticed that when we get money, either as a salary or from some windfall or the other, we often lose our ability to plan for that money?"

"Happens to me all the time," Soma confessed. "I mean, I just got a bonus, and here I am on a shopping spree for clothes, that in retrospect, I really don't need."

"That's what I'm talking about."

"If you don't have a plan for money, once it shows up, we develop some level of amnesia, which usually clears when all the money's gone."

"Tell me about it. Since we started talking, I've felt the scales falling from my eyes and have a huge case of buyer's remorse."

"Don't we all?" laughed Tolu.

And as they laughed, Soma couldn't help but feel helpless as she felt the flood waters of debt swirl around her, pulling her towards poverty with only an umbrella for protection.

While preparing for a rainy day, expect a flood, she pondered.

Tolu wasn't done. She sipped her drink, and continued: "The Life Strategist also said that when it comes to managing rainy days, there are 3 levels of security."

"Pray tell," Soma prodded.

"He said that while the rainy day is guaranteed to come, what isn't guaranteed is the duration of the rain and your level of cover, should it catch you unawares."

"Hmmm. That's deep."

"It was so easy understanding how money works, listening to him. You know how all other 'finance gurus' make money matters seem so complicated. But this guy really dumbed it down for me. I felt like I was reading one of those books 'for dummies' but the good thing was that he did it without making me feel stupid."

"That's so important," Soma concurred. "So what did he say the 3 levels of security are?"

Tolu smiled and took a bite of her ham sandwich. She chewed slowly, savouring every bit.

"Oooooh Tolu! The suspense is killing me." An exasperated Soma pulled her friend's plate out of reach.

Tolu laughed, dabbing her lips. "I just couldn't resist. Okay, I'll tell you."

"You better, if you know what's good for you," Soma grinned.

"Okay. So using the rainy day as a metaphor, he said that there are 3 levels of protection or cover – the shower cap, the umbrella and the boat."

"Hmmm. I'd love to hear what the shower cap is like," Soma smiled.

"That's what I said when I heard him mention it," Tolu smiled back. "Being ladies, the shower cap as we very well know, keeps our hair dry even though the rest of our body parts get wet. It can only be used by one person at a time and does not or cannot provide adequate protection for the wearer, leaving you vulnerable to the elements. So, if your finances are a 'shower cap', when the rainy day comes, you have limited protection for just yourself. Your finances aren't enough to care for another person. You're protected only to the degree of a minimal disaster; anything more and you're going to get soaked, drenched and washed away. What's more, the shower cap cannot carry you, but needs to be carried by you to protect you."

"Oluwa oh!" Soma groaned. "I'm finished".

Tolu paused to let the gravity of her words sink in.

"The umbrella is a little better than the shower cap," she then continued, "even though they both fall into the same category of what the Life Strategist called 'selfie holdings'."

Soma giggled uncontrollably. "Selfie holdings?! What's that?" she asked.

Tolu chuckled.

"I know, right? He said that as long as you have to work for money and your level of security is tied to your physical exertion and input, then you're a selfie holder because your holdings are tied to you."

"Oh my God!" Soma exclaimed. "I'm definitely a selfie holder. That's terrible. What happens if I lose my job today? Dear God, I've been such a fool." She cradled her head in her hands.

"I know the feeling," Tolu said, comforting her friend. "Sometimes, shock therapy is the best cure to get one out of lethargy."

"Chai! This is a rude shock." Soma smiled ruefully, taking a moment for it to sink in. "Tolu, abeg continue."

"Where was I? Ah, yes, the umbrella. As I said before, the umbrella requires your effort to provide you with cover. Now, unlike the shower cap that only provides cover for one person, the umbrella can cover a maximum of three persons – two adults and a small child, which would probably be the size of a young family."

"That's about the size of my family, except I've got two kids," Soma said.

"Exactly," Tolu concurred. "That's the average household. Parents work hard in the present to provide their families a good lifestyle, but are many times, digging ditches of debt in the future. My dear, the umbrella may provide some level of cover, but you're still going to get drenched by the rain, depending on its intensity."

"That's true."

"And besides, there's a kind of downpour that renders an umbrella useless, and makes it fold inside out or fly away," Tolu continued.

"Na true oh!" Soma placed her hand over her mouth.

The analogy hit too close to home. What happens if my umbrella flies away? she thought.

Tolu paused as she observed her friend deep in thought. She reached over and squeezed Soma's hand.

"Soma, I know all I've said seems like a hard pill to swallow, but I've discovered, albeit from bitter personal experience, that no matter how far down a wrong road you've gone, you can always turn around and retrace your steps. You don't have to learn the hard way and make the same mistakes I did."

Soma nodded, sniffing as she dabbed her eye.

"Damn!" she groaned, "I've ruined my mascara. Don't worry about me dear, I'll be fine. Tell me about the boat."

"Okay," Tolu continued. "Unlike the shower cap and the umbrella which depend on your self-exertion and physical input, the boat carries you. And like any boat, it's designed to handle tough conditions. Depending on the size of the boat, it can carry varying numbers of people. The bigger the boat, the better the cover. The boat insulates you from the elements, keeping you dry and more importantly, the boat rides on what others drown in."

"Word. That's deep. The boat rides on what others drown in."

Tolu nodded. "Just like in biblical times, Noah was warned by God to prepare for a flood, so he spent a long time, building a boat - the ark. His friends and neighbors laughed at him, because it seemed like a ridiculous thing to do, especially since there had never been rain before that time. Eventually, when the rainy day came, it was such a deluge that everyone began to run towards what Noah had taken years to build. Luckily for Noah, his boat could cover himself, his wife, their three sons, their wives and a couple of hundred pets too, while everyone else, sadly, got washed away."

Soma sighed. It was all beginning to make so much sense.

"The Life Strategist said that having a boat provides trans-generational cover and security. That's the kind of wealth that trust funds are made of." Tolu grinned as she sipped her drink.

"Yes oh!" Soma exclaimed. "I've read the story of Noah before, but I've never actually seen it from a financial perspective before now."

"So the big question is 'how covered are you?' When the rain falls, what sort of protection will you have?" Tolu asked.

Soma replied quickly. "Cover ke? Me wey never even get shower cap sef. If rain fall, my own don finish be dat."

"I feel you my sister. This was such a wake-up call for me too. Like the Life Strategist said, if you save for a rainy day, you might get a flood; so you might as well save for a flood and breeze through the rainy days."

Soma couldn't help but agree.

Don't prepare for the rainy day. Prepare for a flood and the rainy day will take care of itself.

TOTAL MONEY WORKOUT

1. What opportunities have you missed out on?
2. What opportunities have you taken advantage of lately?
3. How covered are you? Do you have a shower cap, umbrella or boat?
4. When the rain falls, what sort of protection will you have?

CHAPTER THREE

WHERE IS YOUR EMPIRE?

Secret 3: If God gave it to you for free, you can earn a fee for it.

SATURDAY
HOME
3:00pm

Here's my card, give me a call sometime. Perhaps we can get you off the broad road where many are unfortunately on their way to financial ruin, onto the straight and narrow of financial fitness, where some of us reside.

Toks' words had been on replay on Ezzy's mind since their discussion at The Lounge.

Financial ruin or financial mastery? Ezzy thought. "To be or not to be? That is the question," Ezzy muttered, quoting a line from Shakespeare's Hamlet.

At the same time, Soma was deep in thought.

What use is an umbrella when you're drowning in a flood? Tolu's words had also been reverberating through her mind.

“We need to talk,” they both said at the same time.

“Jinx!” Soma laughed. “You're not allowed to speak until I say your name,” she continued.

This used to be one of our favourite games, she rued. *What's happened to us?*

Even as she pondered, she realized the answer. *Whoever said that the love of money was the root of all evil was mistaken. It's the lack of money that's the root of all evil.*

Soma turned to Ezzy, slowly tracing her finger down his spine, up through his shoulder blades and through his dark, frizzy hair.

“Now that I have your undivided attention,” she began; he flinched as her fingers worked their way down his hairy chest. “I've been thinking. I bumped into Tolu, my former colleague, at the shopping mall the other day and she gave me more than enough food for thought. We earn quite a good living, are able to afford some of the good things life has to offer, but we're barely getting by. It seems that at the end of the month, there's a long queue of bills to pay that by the time we're done, we're living from hand to mouth. I really don't think that's wise.”

Ezzy was about to speak when Soma hushed him. “I don't believe I gave you the permission to speak, did I?” She said, slowly circling his chair.

Ezzy shook his head.

“As I was saying before that rude interruption, we need to begin some major debt cancellation efforts as well as significantly increase our sources of income if we're to ever get on the road to recovery,” Soma finished.

Ezzy raised his hand.

“Now you may address the court, Mr. Ezekiel,” she chuckled.

“Thank you, Your Honour. I was about to agree with the prosecution's claim that we need to revise our financial standing as I also bumped into an old friend who gave me quite the eye-opener.”

"Well, I guess it's a sign or a warning and we better take heed."

"Here we go again," Ezzy sneered, "superstitious wife on the loose."

"Come off it, Ezekiel, I'm serious," Soma begged.

"So am I," he replied. "Toks gave me his card, and by all estimations, he seemed to know what he was talking about and not to mention, he's doing pretty well for himself; it won't hurt to pick his brain a little."

"Let's schedule a meeting for the weekend," Soma suggested.

"I'll call him up right away."

SUNDAY
CASA DE TOKS
3:00pm

"Sorry for barging in on your Sunday weekend on such short notice," Ezzy apologized as Toks ushered them into an expansive lounge.

Man, this is the life! Ezzy thought as he looked around Toks' living room. *This living room should be featured on MTV's Cribs.*

"Don't sweat it. You're more than welcome." Toks smiled as he walked them through the foyer.

"So what do I get you guys to drink?" he asked.

"Nothing, I'm fine," said Soma.

"Some wine would be fine," Ezzy said, totally oblivious of Soma's penetrating glare. She'd insisted he stop drinking, but apparently, her husband still had love for the fruit of the vine.

Toks signaled to his housekeeper as he reclined into a plush, comfortable leather sofa. "Wine for the gentleman and some juice for the lady.

"Soma, you look as radiant as always."

Soma blushed at Toks' compliment. "Thanks, Toks. That's very kind of you."

Turning to his friend, Toks launched in. "So tell me Ezzy, what's going on?"

Ezzy began: "Well, you remember the conversation we had at The Lounge a few weeks ago where you were talking about finding Aladdin's magic lamp; you know, talking about financial fitness. I mean, bro, look at you. You've got it real good and despite the uncertain imbalances in the economy, your business keeps growing in leaps and bounds. I see you diversifying your business interests and all. I open the newspapers, and there you are doing something great; I turn on the TV, and there's something or the other about your exploits. You're definitely having the time of your life.

"But on the flip side, look at me. I'm working a dead-end job, barely getting by, and my 'take home pay' doesn't even take me home. My kids go to some really expensive schools and I fight tooth and nail to keep them there. I have a pretty good home and two nice cars but I'm buried deep in debt and I have no investments. I'm of no societal significance and apart from my family, the only person that cares about me is the barkeeper at The Lounge – and all he cares about are the tips I give him." Ezzy paused and smiled ruefully.

"So tell me, Toks, how do you do it? What's your secret?"

Toks heard the frustration in Ezzy's words and saw the anguish in Soma's eyes as her tears began to well up and slide down her cheeks. He'd seen the same scenario repeat itself several times before, with different couples.

So he began.

"Ezzy, Soma, listen to me. I've known you guys for a long time and I'm going to level with you. I'm going to share several hard truths with you and I hope you can swallow these bitter pills?"

Ezzy and Soma nodded. Anything that Toks had to share would be better than this two-faced existence they were currently living.

“Go ahead Toks,” Soma implored.

“The first thing you need to realize is that God has wired each and every person with certain gifts, talents, abilities and skill sets to function in what I call its place of instinct.”

“Place of instinct? Sounds like a programme on Discovery Cha-- Ouch!” Ezzy screamed as Soma dug her well-manicured nails into his thigh, effectively shutting up his intended joke. Her husband had a misplaced sense of humour and now wasn't the time to act the fool.

“I'm sorry, Toks, please continue,” Soma apologized, glaring at her husband.

“Yeah, Toks, I'm sorry,” Ezzy took the cue, rubbing his throbbing thigh.

“It's okay. As I said before, every individual was created by God and given instincts to perform optimally in their particular environment. Give you an instance; take a look at the eagle. Though it shares several anatomical similarities with other birds, it's unique. It's got keen vision, an incredible wingspan, claws and soars even in the storm. But where's its instinctive environment?”

“The air,” Soma and Ezzy chorused.

“Absolutely! Next, let's look at the fish. What environment does it perform instinctively? Obviously, it goes without saying that it's in the water. Now, I don't know about you, but I can categorically say that fish don't fly, do they?”

“No they don't. But you should see--” Ezzy paused as he felt Soma's fingers climbing up his trouser leg. “Never mind. Do continue,” he winced as Soma pinched him again.

Toks smiled. Soma definitely had his old friend in check.

“As I was saying, every creature was designed to succeed in its instinctive environment. Birds are equipped with the tools to flourish in flight; fish were also naturally designed with the gills and fins that aid swimming. In the same vein, each human was given specific gifts, talents, abilities and skill sets to function optimally in a particular field that comes instinctively to them. I mean, think about it. Birds don't go to flight school and fish don't take swimming lessons either, but their gifts are expressed instinctively. It's our responsibility to find out what we're instinctively wired to do and be fired up all our lives to get it done!"

Toks paused as he let his words take effect. He looked at Ezzy whose furrowed brow spoke volumes of what he was thinking and then glanced at Soma as she scribbled furiously in her notepad.

Soma pondered as she wrote the question on her notepad, *where's my place of instinct?*

Toks continued: "So how do you discover your place of instinct or what you're wired for? Well, there are a few pointers that I discovered after graduating from the university."

Ezzy and Soma leaned forward.

"The first step in uncovering your instinct is to ask yourself, 'what skill comes to me naturally or with ease?' The sad fact of life is that too many people despise their gift or abilities, regarding them as commonplace or worse still, they deem them as being nothing of significant value, forgetting that people don't pay for talent, they pay for skill or products. So your talent or perceived lack of talent really isn't the issue; it's only the foundation on which you can begin to build a superstructure that can house your giftings."

"Hmm," Ezzy sighed. Toks' words, though simple, seemed to make a lot of sense. He cast a glance at Soma, who was clearly lost in thought. "Come on Toks, it really can't be that easy. Dude, there are millions of people out there with some kind of talent. I mean, talents and gifts come a dime a dozen. So why doesn't having talent or some kind of special ability guarantee success?"

Toks smiled. He'd heard so many people make the same excuse so many times before.

"Ezzy, my brother, here's something you need to recognize. It's not what you don't have that limits you; it's what you have, but don't know how to use."

"Toks, you're so full of parables. Perhaps you should consider a career as a motivational speaker."

Soma scowled. She couldn't believe that her husband could be so flippant and cavalier. "Toks, please don't pay your friend any attention," she apologized. "You know how he can be. His jokes often have the poor taste of bad timing.

"Ezzy, what's wrong with you?! We came to Toks to learn from the wealth of his experience and now you're acting up. Would we be able to afford his time if we had to pay for it? The least we can do is listen. After all, he has the results to show for it," she snapped.

Ezzy froze.

He couldn't remember the last time he'd heard Soma speak to him with such rage and vitriol. And then it dawned on him. All these years, he had been giving *reasons* for his failures instead of *results* of his success.

Do I have reasons or results? he thought. He knew the answer.

"I'm sorry, Tokunbo. I guess my familiarity with you got in the way of my learning from you. It's not easy for me. I mean, we went to school together, served together during our Youth Corps and now, give or take 18 years, I'm broke, busted and absolutely disgusted; while from what I've seen and heard, you're well on your way to being a billionaire. It just doesn't seem fair," Ezzy wailed.

"Ezzy, I totally understand. I know it can't be easy for you to fathom, especially since we have a lot of history together, that's why I'm not holding anything back, but I'm sharing with you what I learned from the bitter swill of my experience.

"Ezzy, Soma, I need you guys to listen to me very clearly," Toks continued. "You cannot receive from whom you don't respect."

"Nooooo! Toks, please don't think that. We respect you." Soma knelt on the parquet floor.

"I know, Soma, please get up." He waited until she was seated again before he continued. "I'm not referring to myself. You cannot receive wealth if and when you have no respect for money.

"Money is like a very beautiful woman, she naturally has many suitors. Everyone wants to get with her. Some have a 'one night stand', where they get a 'breakthrough' and eventually are worse off than they were before they met her. Others want a fling, where they have an occasional affair with success, but don't have what it takes to commit fully. Most want to use her, but always get dumped by her. But have you noticed? Fewer people have a permanent arrangement with her.

"She must be courted…on her terms. You must be able to get her attention and when you do, treat her special, but let her know her place. If you esteem her too highly, perhaps to the point of worship, she turns into a dominatrix and makes you endure all sorts of painful contortions until she gets rid of you. Treat her like a tramp and she'll never enter your home. You must have a vision, a plan of action and a system that works for her that would cause her to want to move in with you and give you the family of wealth that you so desire."

"That's how I got Soma to marry me!" Ezzy laughed while Soma giggled and punched him playfully on the shoulder.

The laughter was a good ice breaker.

"Okay, so back to the subject of passion, purpose and finding your natural habitat; there are a few pointers to look out for." Toks reached for a glass of orange juice.

"Let me put it this way. You were created and designed to succeed in a type of environment, habitat or kingdom. Your purpose is to *find your empire* or the area that you were created to have dominion over. That's the first step. Unfortunately, most people never get to the first step because they think their 'empire' is insignificant, thus they despise it. But guess what? The fact that you are born in a kingdom doesn't make you a king."

"Hmm. True talk," Soma muttered. What she was learning was so profound that she turned on the recorder app on her phone and began recording.

"The second step," Toks continued, "where we separate the men from the boys, is where you *establish your authority.* Here, you've worked your gift so hard and consistently that you begin to get recognized as a king or authority in that field. Here, people begin to recognize you as a solution provider as your name begins to stand for something - it is building a brand or following due to your track record.

"Here, you're not dealing with talent alone, but you've honed your gift into a skill that serves you without fail. Recognize that it was David's understanding and skill as a military strategist that caused him to lead Israel successfully through battle, without ever losing; all this before he was crowned as king.

"Hold on a sec, I know you probably don't have your Bibles here. Let me read it to you."

Toks reached for his iPad and opened the Bible app. "Here we are," he said.

> *"All the tribes of Israel came to David at Hebron and said, we are your own flesh and blood. In the past, while Saul was king over us, YOU were the one who led Israel on their military campaigns. – (2nd Samuel 5:2).*

"So as you can see, the entire nation recognized David's skill and authority as a leader even though he was not yet king."

"Sorry to interrupt you, Toks, but do you mean I could be a king if I'm constantly recognized as a solution provider to a specific problem that some of my friends have?" Soma asked.

"Exactly!" concurred Toks.

"The reason I ask this is because every time my friends have a party, event, function or get-together, they would usually ask me to provide catering services for the event; they say I'm pretty good at it, but I've never taken catering or culinary courses," Soma said excitedly.

"Fantastic!" Toks clapped. "Now you get it."

"But hold on a second, Soma. Do you get paid for those services?" Toks asked, with a mischievous glint in his eye.

"No, Toks, I don't. I enjoy it so much that I could do it for free," Soma replied.

"You've just hit the nail on the head, my dear," Toks said excitedly. "Now listen to me, both of you. What I'm about to say is perhaps the most important thing I've said so far. Soma, you're going to need to write this down."

With that, Soma reached for her notepad and pen.

"We're listening, Toks," Ezzy said.

The suspense was so thick; you could cut it with a knife.

"If God gave it to you for free, you can earn a fee for it."

"Word!" Ezzy thumped his fist on the arm of the leather sofa. He repeated the words slowly, "If God gave it to you for free, you can earn a fee for it."

"Now I get it!" he exclaimed. "Toks, that's why the world's most successful people in every field are less than 5% of the general population; they get paid to do what comes to them naturally! They get paid to do what they love! It's ridiculously simple! I mean, look at Oprah, she gets paid to have conversations with people; but long before there was an Oprah show, she was a reporter, it was her conversational gift that was being perfected all that time."

Ezzy couldn't help himself; it was as obvious as the nose on his face.

"That's it, Ezzy. The list is endless. Richard Branson today, is a billionaire and serial entrepreneur, but he started his first business venture, *Student* magazine while still a teenager. Today, the *Virgin* brand manages over 300 businesses. Bill Gates is synonymous with computers and Information Technology, but most people don't know that when he was about 10 years old, he would spend hours in front of the school's only computer, which at that time, was the size of a small room. When school was over, he would sneak back into school when he was meant to be asleep and hack into the computer and write programs until morning, then he would sneak back home. He did this until he was eventually discovered when the computer finally ran out of scheduled units of time. He got admitted into Harvard, unarguably, the world's most prestigious university to study Law, but dropped out to pursue his lifelong passion for computers, and today, the rest, they say, is history."

Toks paused.

"What is the common thread that binds these three individuals?" he asked.

"They dropped out of school!" Ezzy smiled.

"Close, but no cigar. Try again, wise guy." Toks smirked.

"They've learned how to profit from their passion and created a business structure around it." Soma jumped excitedly.

"Is that your final answer?" Toks grinned, imitating Frank Edoho, the host of the popular TV show, "Who Wants To Be A Millionaire".

"Final answer." Soma clapped in excitement.

"Drumroll please?" Toks asked as Ezzy tapped his fingers on the glass table beside him.

Pausing to heighten the suspense, Toks exclaimed, "Congratulations Soma, you've won our Grand prize!"

As Ezzy and Soma hugged each other in celebration, Toks reached for his glass, sipped his drink and smiled.

They had begun their total money workout.

TOTAL MONEY WORKOUT

1. Have you discovered your place of instinct? What comes to you naturally? What are you wired and fired for?
2. Have you been giving reasons for failure?
3. What are the usual excuses you give for failure or lack of achievement?
4. Are there people in your circle whose success you resent? Be honest. Write their names down and why you resent them.
5. Describe your relationship with money as honestly as possible.
6. What problem should people have for your name to be the solution?
7. What could you earn a fee for that you're currently doing for free?

CHAPTER FOUR

SIT YOUR MONEY

Secret 4: "True wealth is not determined by how much you earn, but by how much you keep"

"Soma, have I got a surprise for you!" Amaka cooed as she sauntered towards Soma's desk.

"What elaborate scheme have you planned out now, Amaka?" Soma smiled.

"Shoes!" Amaka whispered conspiratorially. "I've got the latest fashions. Jimmy Choo, Gucci, Prada and I even got that shoe that we saw in the last edition of Marie Claire," she smiled proudly.

"No! For real?" Soma looked around. "Let me take a look."

Amaka glanced around furtively and handed Soma 'the package', who immediately stashed it underneath her table.

"Wow!" she gasped. "This is the exact one that Kim Kardashian wore to the MET Gala."

"I told you I'd get it if I wanted it." Amaka smiled proudly. "And it can all be yours for the paltry sum of one hundred and thirty-five thousand naira. And for a further bargain, you can pay in two installments."

Amaka waited. She knew that Soma had an incurable shoe fetish. There was no way she could resist.

Soma paused.

She could already smell the new leather, the heel was the right length and best of all, she had the perfect bag to go with it.

Soma took a deep breath and muttered, "Walk away, all you've got to do is say no".

"Soma, are you speaking in tongues? What's taking you so long?"

"I'm sorry, babe," Soma sighed. "I won't be able to buy these shoes yet. I didn't plan for it in my budget this month, maybe I'll be able to get it next month."

"Huh?" Amaka couldn't believe her ears. "Budget? Soma, are you high? You practically bullied me into buying these shoes and now you're talking about a budget?"

"I'm sorry, Amy," Soma pleaded. "You wouldn't understand."

"Fimile jo! Next time, you'll see if I'll answer you. Budget ke! Budget nini! Biko hafum aka!"

And with that, she stormed off.

Soma, on the other hand, was in shock. She couldn't believe that she had just turned down the opportunity to buy shoes.

Not just run-of-the-mill shoes, designer shoes.

But not just any designer shoes, Christian Louboutin shoes. Red bottoms.

But deep inside, she couldn't help but feel that she was doing the right thing. But why did it hurt so bad?

Staying disciplined to this financial plan was going to be a lot harder than she thought.

Across town, Ezzy was going through his own personal debacle.

"Earth to Ezekiel, do you read me?" Hassan asked as Ezzy seemed lost in deep thought."Hellooooooo?! Ezzy, what the heck is going on?

"Okay, if you can't loan me 200K, I can settle for 150K, I'm sure that I can rustle up the remaining 50K from one of the guys, but at least, say something; don't play deaf."

"Sorry, bro, kinda zoned out for a moment. What did you want?" Ezzy asked.

"Are you for real?" Hassan couldn't believe what he was hearing.

"I've been sitting in front of you for at least five minutes asking for a loan and you mean to tell me that you didn't hear one word of what I said?" He fumed.

"Sorry, bro. Like I said, had a lot on my mind," apologized Ezzy.

"Okay, okay! All's forgiven, as soon as you write me a cheque for 200K." Hassan smiled.

"Two hundred what? Dude, are you insane? I definitely don't have that kind of money lying around!" yelled Ezzy in consternation.

"Of course, you do." countered Hassan. "Come on Ezekiel, it's no secret that you're one of the biggest, I daresay the biggest rainmaker this firm has ever had; and you make some tidy profits from the commissions you get off the jobs you source for the firm. By my estimation, you've cleaned out to the tune of at least three million over the last seven months, so bro, leave story. There's no way that you can tell me that you've blown all that money." Hassan ended his argument with the flourish and satisfied grin of a prosecutor who knew that he had just won the case and was just waiting for the jury to rule in his favor.

Ezzy couldn't answer. Hassan was right; he'd earned in excess of N3.5 million and if truth be told, he had 'blown the money'.

What had he done with it all?

I've been such a fool, he thought.

"What a stupid life I've lived." He turned his swivel chair and looked out of the window, now totally oblivious of Hassan's presence.

Ezzy and Soma had good cause to worry. They'd previously had a Total Money Workout coaching session with Toks.

It hadn't gone so well.

Soma and Ezzy sat quietly as they waited for Toks' verdict. It felt eerily reminiscent of being in the principal's office awaiting sentencing for bad behavior.

"Hmm," Toks sighed. Their finances didn't look too great.

"I know it's bad, Toks. But it really can't be that bad, can it?" Ezzy asked hopefully.

"You're right," Toks replied. "It's not that bad, it's worse."

Ezzy was crestfallen.

"I'm going to level with you guys. Your financial state leaves a lot to be desired. You've made a lot of pretty irresponsible and reckless decisions and you're drowning in a flood of debt and barely holding on to a thin branch for support, and if you're not careful, you're going to go under."

Toks wasn't about to baby them. He'd seen too many good people lose their homes, and leave their children destitute because of poor financial decisions.

"Okay guys, this is what we're going to do. We're going to take it from the top and begin at the basics.

"True wealth is not determined by how much you earn, but by how much you keep."

"That's true," Soma concurred. "I've realized that even though I earn a good income, for some strange reason, my take-home pay doesn't take me home."

Ezzy agreed.

"And do you know why that is?" Toks asked.

"Umm..." Ezzy scratched his head, searching for the answer.

"I'll tell you," Toks continued. "If you don't have a plan for money, money will have a plan for you."

"Hmm!" Ezzy and Soma said in unison. They couldn't agree more.

"Ezzy, do you remember what I told you at The Lounge several weeks ago? I asked you to imagine money as a servant, ready to do your bidding. It often comes at the time of the month you receive your pay check; and when it does, it expects you to have a planned schedule of activities or duties you require it to perform, which is called a budget. If you can provide that budget, money defers to you and becomes your servant; but if you're unable to provide one, money turns the tables on you and automatically becomes your master."

"Yeah, I remember." Ezzy sighed. "I definitely felt like I was a slave to money."

Toks continued. "What you need to realize is that wealth is first a mindset. There are a few fundamental differences between rich people and poor people and it first starts in their mind before it takes place in their lives as an action.

"Don't forget that the Good Book says, as a man thinks in his heart..."

"So is he!" chorused Ezzy and Soma.

"Let me put it into perspective," Toks continued. "First, let's get the meaning of POOR. It's an acronym for – Passing Over Opportunities Repeatedly. Now a—"

"Tweetable!" Soma grinned, her notepad materializing.

"POOR – Passing Over Opportunities Repeatedly."

Toks smiled, then continued. "Now a poor thinking man uses his hard-earned income or salary to buy liabilities, while a rich thinking man uses his income to buy assets, which give him returns and then, those returns pay for his liabilities."

"Man, Toks, that's hitting too close to home," Ezzy moaned.

"Wow!" Soma muttered under her breath. Now, I know why we're poor.

"Though it sounds simple enough, you'd be surprised to know that most people don't know the difference between assets and liabilities," Toks continued.

"That's odd." Soma replied. "An asset is anything you buy that appreciates in value, while a liability is anything you buy that depreciates in value."

"I knew you'd say that," Toks countered, "but that's the school book definition.

"An asset is anything that puts money into your pocket, while a liability is anything that takes money from your pocket. So let's look at a few examples of assets and liabilities shall we?

"The car you own and drive; asset or liability?" Toks asked.

"Liability!" Soma and Ezzy chorused.

"Fantastic! Ten points," smiled Toks.

"Next question. The car you bought but use for hire; asset or liability?" Toks asked.

"Asset!" chorused the couple.

This was fun. The last few days they had spent together on their Total Money Workout had brought them closer in ways they hadn't experienced for a long while. Ezzy high-fived his wife. The lack of money is truly the root of evil, he thought.

Toks interrupted his reverie. "Moving on. What would you call your rented apartment? An asset or liability?"

"A liability!" they yelled.

"Ten points to the couple in the blue corner.

"Now for my final question. You have a total of thirty points. If you get this right, you win the game. But if you get it wrong, you lose all your points and you go back to zero."

Toks had definitely watched too many episodes of the popular game show, "Who Wants To Be A Millionaire". Ezzy and Soma steeled themselves for the final question.

"What would you call the house that you build and live in? Is it an asset or a liability?

"Wait!" Toks yelled.

Ezzy and Soma froze. They'd never heard Toks use such a firm tone before. "You must agree and answer as a team," he said. "Any answer that's given will be taken as the team's answer."

Ezzy spoke up. "Sure thing boss, we're ready."

They steeled themselves as Toks asked the question again: "What would you call the house that you build and live in? Is it an asset or a liability?"

Toks watched as Soma whispered into Ezzy's ear and smiled as Ezzy shook his head determinedly and rubbed his palms with glee.

"Don't worry Soma, I got this!"

"Okay." Toks looked deadpan.

"The house that you build and live in is an asset!" Ezzy cheered, with a triumphant look on his face.

"Is that your final answer?" Toks asked, still deadpan.

For a brief moment, Ezzy seemed unsure, but it didn't last long. His cheeky grin soon replaced any doubt. "Final answer."

Toks paused dramatically. The suspense in the room was so tangible, you could cut it with a knife.

Ezzy was right, Soma thought smiling, Tokunbo had definitely watched too many episodes of the popular gameshow.

"The house that you build to live in is..."

Ezzy could feel little beads of perspiration beginning to form on his brow.

"The house that you build to live in is NOT an asset!"

Soma punched Ezzy on the shoulder. "Shey I told you?" she growled at him and pinched his arm.

"I'm sorry, you've lost all your points and have crashed to Ground Zero. Better luck next time, guys," Toks said with an air of finality.

"Noooo! Tokunbo, I disagree with you." Ezzy yelled. "How can you say that the house we build and live in is a liability? After all, if we have our own home, we cease being at the mercy of a landlord; the money we would have paid him can now be channeled into our own property. On this particular issue, I vehemently disagree!"

Toks smiled. He'd heard this spiel a thousand times from people he had to educate during his Total Money Workout sessions.

"Ezzy, I understand your argument. While it's a valid one, it doesn't quite pan out that way. You see, while I agree that you're no longer at the mercy of your landlord, you transfer the money you would have paid him into the coffers of the State through taxes, surveys, land use charges and other expenses, which include building costs, maintenance fees, etc."

Ezzy frowned, still unconvinced.

Toks smiled. "Just stay with me a second and have an open mind."

Ezzy relaxed. After all, Tokunbo being a dollar multi-millionaire, had results he could only dream of.

"Another argument I've heard in favor of a house being an asset is the fact that it can be used as collateral to secure a loan. Now don't forget the definition of an asset as anything that puts money into your pocket. Therefore your house is not an asset unless you put it up for sale, and until then, it earns no income. Besides, are all houses loan worthy? Definitely not. So, while your house can be used as security for a loan to the bank, your home is classified as a risk asset, therefore, corroborating and consolidating its status as a liability. Now you'll probably throw in the argument that your house can appreciate in value, right?"

"Ehen now."

"But if you had built a house, say a block of four flats and you'd put three of those flats up for rent while you lived in one flat, how many assets do you have?"

"Three assets," Ezzy acquiesced. It was slowly beginning to make sense.

"Remember what we said about the poor and rich thinking people?" Toks asked.

"Yeah? What about them?" Ezzy returned.

"Have you forgotten so soon? A poor thinking man uses his hard-earned income or salary to buy liabilities, while a rich thinking man uses his income to buy assets, which give him returns and then, those returns pay for his liabilities. In conclusion, your house will only be considered as an asset if it earns income for you or if your returns are so significant that it can fund such a liability."

"Toks, if you don't mind my asking, how do we manage the little financial drops that make a mighty ocean?"

"That's a great question, Soma and I'm glad you asked," Toks smiled. "You've got to learn how to SIT your money."

"Sit?" chorused Ezzy and Soma.

"Absolutely!" continued Toks. "SIT is an acronym for Savings, Investments and Tithe."

"Nice one," smiled Ezzy. "You've always had a way with words."

"Thanks, bro." Toks smiled and continued.

"A SIT plan is an imperative tool in designing and sticking to your budget. And as you know now, money must be planned for before it shows up. Now from what I see from your Total Money Workout score, your money's in pretty bad shape and the reason is largely due to the fact that you haven't mastered your money. After we've dealt with that, we'll deal with your debt – we need to close the tap before we mop the floor."

"So how does it work?" Soma asked.

"It's really quite simple," Toks replied. "You're going to need your trusty notepad for this."

Soma reached for it.

"Let's assume we're preparing for next month's salary, that's July. Remember I said you've got to prepare for money before it shows up. Now I need you to draw a table."

Soma did as she was told.

"Now, on top of that table, please write July. I need you to label the left side of the table as Breakdown and the right side, Amount. Let's continue. Now on the Breakdown side, I need you to write S on one row, I on the next row, and finally, T on the third row. Conversely, I need you to go to the Amount column and place the following values for the SIT rows; 20% for the S row, 20% for the I row and 10% for the T row."

Breakdown	Amount %
S	20
I	20
T	10
TOTAL:	50 (DO NOT TOUCH)
Recurrent Expenditure	
DSTV	
Entertainment	
Groceries	
etc	

Soma scribbled furiously.

"As you've probably noticed, these values on the *Amount* column add up to 50%. Now, this is pretty steep and I often don't advise that recent converts to the Total Money Workout lifestyle make that quantum leap so quickly. As a wise man once said, '*if you go up before you grow up, when you get up, you'll mess up; but if you go up to grow up, when you get up, you'll stay up*'."

"Dude, I'm serious, you've definitely got a way with words, you could be a rapper and I could be your manager and we could go on tour and get sponsors--"

Toks laughed. "I think those days are far behind me, but let's get back to the issue at hand."

"No wahala, but if you change your mind, holla at your boy and I'll hook you up. I've got a friend who can hook us up with Don Jazzy". Ezzy was incorrigible.

"Sure thing." Toks smiled.

"As I was saying, I wouldn't suggest that you begin with such a steep investment. I would recommend that you take baby steps first, crawl next until you gain the confidence to stand and eventually race to financial freedom."

"So what's your recommendation?" Ezzy asked.

"Start simple. You might want to start your Savings and Investments at 5% each and your Tithe, constant at 10%. Now don't be fooled, it's easier said than done. Many good intentions get sacrificed on the altar of indiscipline. If you can't pass the test of discipline that is stage one, I guarantee that you won't pass stage two. Let me also inform you that money has a routine, she won't let you change it by your mere whim for Financial Freedom, she's used to being in charge, and making all the decisions, so she's going to resist you at every twist and turn, so don't expect it to be an easy ride."

"Ezzy, I'm scared." There was a slight tremble in Soma's voice.

"I am too, dear," admitted Ezzy. "But we're in good hands with Tokunbo, aren't we Toks?"

"Indeed you are, guys, and I'm proud of you both. It takes a lot of courage to delay gratification and face your demons." Toks smiled.

"Back to the SIT plan. As you can see, you now have a SIT total of 20%. That's what I like to call *Do Not Touch Money.* Under no circumstance, save a natural disaster and the reason for which you put it aside are you allowed to touch that money. Listen guys, most people have *savings accounts*, but have no *savings* in those accounts."

"That sounds like us," muttered Soma.

"Do you know why people find themselves in that predicament?" Toks asked.

Ezzy spoke up. "Well, I think it's because they didn't prepare and plan adequately for using money."

"That's right." Toks continued, "but in addition to that, the reason behind that is because their savings accounts are not given names."

"Not given names? I'm sorry, Toks, I'm afraid I don't follow," Soma said.

"Let me explain, my dear. Names are very important because they serve to give identity to the persons and the things around us. In business, the term, savings is used quite generically. Money must be put on an assignment, that's why it comes...to serve you. Now, while most people would readily admit to having a savings account, fewer people can point to any significant income lodged within those accounts. I believe that it was Dr. Myles Munroe that said, *when a purpose of a thing is not known, abuse is inevitable."*

"That's true, Toks, but what has that got to do with having a savings account?" Soma asked.

"Elementary, my dear Soma," Toks replied as he poured them a drink.

"You see, my dear, if you don't know what a savings account is created for, you will abuse it. As far as I'm concerned, it is a great tool to protect your money on a project basis. You see, Soma, to most people, that account is where the leftovers go; it's where they go with their ATM's to have easy access to cash to fulfill any and every whim that comes their way. Remember that I said that money must be given an assignment; also, there are no limits or restrictions to the number of savings accounts you can operate. Let me tell you what I do. I have come to believe that if your account is not named, any name can take the money."

Ezzy and Soma looked blank.

"I'll make it easier on you. If your savings account is called *No Name*, it means *Any Name* can access it. Are you with me so far?" Toks asked.

"So far, so good." Ezzy grinned.

Toks continued: "Now because your savings account has no name, which means that it was not set up for any specific purpose, any need you have e.g. fuel, treats, getting nice Brazilian hair extensions, expensive gifts, etc. will naturally have a reason to eat up your savings."

"True," Ezzy concurred.

"So what I do is to spread my savings into several named *project* accounts e.g. Rent, Holidays, Children's School Fees, Personal Business, etc. And because there's no limit to the number of savings accounts you can operate, you can have as many accounts as there are banks. Now what this does for me is to instill a sense of discipline to managing my finances. Therefore, using the Children's School Fees account as an example, I can only make withdrawals from that account *for the purpose* for which it was created. I know it sounds easier said than done, but that's where discipline kicks in. You've always got to ask yourself; how badly do I want this change?"

"That makes a lot of sense, Toks, but what happens after the *Do Not Touch* section, you know there are living expenses that need to be taken care of."

"That's a fantastic question, Soma. I'm glad you brought it up. After the *Do Not Touch* segment, you must begin to include your recurrent expenditure, which, simply put, are your monthly spending expenses. This would probably include your electricity bills, cable bills, groceries, shopping, entertainment, feeding, etc. You must be able to prepare for those bills before they arrive. And finally, you must set some money aside for what I call *miscellaneous expenses.* Now, here's the Koko of the matter. You are not allowed to purchase whatever is not on your *SIT* plan."

"Hey babe, that means you can't buy that Louis Vuitton bag you've been ogling that's on sale at the Mall since you haven't planned for it." Ezzy smirked as he nudged his scowling wife.

"I'm off the hook," he cheered.

"Leave me joor!" she retorted.

"But I'm afraid that's true, my dear. If you hadn't pre-planned that Louis Vuitton bag into your budget or if it can't be financed by your *miscellaneous expenses*, then you have to delay gratification to a further time."

"I guess I can live without it for now, knowing I have company."

"Company? What company?" Ezzy looked confused as Soma's smile got wider.

"You, dear; this also means that you won't be getting your long-awaited iPhone X. You didn't think I'd forget, did you?"

"Cheeeet," Ezzy muttered.

"Touché!" cheered Toks as he raised his glass to Soma. He smirked at Ezzy, "cheer up, bro. Once you understand the principle and form it into a conscious habit and eventually a lifestyle, your assets will be able to get you as many iPhone's as you desire."

"That would be something, wouldn't it?" Ezzy smiled as he gazed wistfully into the distance.

Toks continued.

"Now, let's not put the cart before the horse. It's the principle that produces the results. Now, if you look at your *SIT* plan, you'd notice something really interesting..."

Ezzy and Soma peered into her notepad.

"Can't seem to see anything out of the ordinary," Ezzy remarked.

Soma concurred. "Neither do I, Toks, what is it?" she asked.

"Your *SIT* plan shows so much money leaving your system!"

Ezzy and Soma didn't get it.

"Okay. Let me break it down again. On the *Do Not Touch* section of your *SIT* plan, you remember we agreed that money no longer belonged to you, since it was particularly for investment purposes of a spiritual and temporal nature."

"Yes," they chorused.

"Also, if you look at the budget section below the *Do Not Touch* section, you'll notice that money is also leaving your system to pay bills and other recurrent expenditure. So that leaves you with nothing! You now have the responsibility of injecting more funds into the system so you don't go broke.

"So let me put it like this, the best your *SIT* plan does for you is to keep you afloat, without it, you're guaranteed to go bust! I like to think of the *SIT* plan like an anchor, holding the boat firm to the ocean floor, though the storms will rage and the waves surge, while the boat may sway from time to time, because it is anchored, it never leaves its moorings."

Soma reached for Ezzy's hand.

"Life happens, guys, but never fear, you're already on the right path. Most families have their financial ship dashed and broken against the rocks of poor decision making and once it begins to capsize, have little less than a twig to hold on to for dear life."

We're dangerously close to crashing, Ezzy thought. *I hope we can turn this boat around.*

Toks continued, "There's an important principle that we seem to have neglected."

"Neglected?" Ezzy asked. "Seems to me that we've covered all the bases."

"All, save one that we merely glossed over as most people do," Toks replied.

Soma looked through her notes and found the missing piece of the puzzle. "Tithing!"

"Oops!" Ezzy murmured. "The terrible T word."

"So here's the moment of truth, guys, do you tithe?" Toks inquired.

Ezzy and Soma fidgeted nervously, looked at each other and then gazed firmly on the floor.

"I'm guessing from your body language, that the answer's no." He smiled.

"Well, not exactly..." Soma tried to explain, quite embarrassed. "It was easy at the beginning, when I wasn't earning so much and my tithes were five thousand naira or so. But the more I earned, the harder it became to give to God. I started to second-guess myself and eventually gave up on giving."

"I like that," Toks said. "*Gave up on giving.*

"And what does the gentleman have to say for himself?" Toks asked Ezzy who was sneaking off towards the bathroom.

"Who, me?" he asked.

"That would be you, bro. So what's your reason for not tithing?" asked Toks.

"Dude, let me not lie to you. I just don't understand it and besides, I think it's a sharp move used by pastors to fleece their flock – no pun intended – so that they can get high on the people's hard-earned supply," Ezzy said.

"I understand you bro, really, I do. But the fact that some abuse the principle for selfish gain does not in itself, invalidate the principle."

"Be that as it may, I'm not sure you can convince me otherwise." Ezzy refused to budge.

"I won't try to," Toks replied. "But all I ask is that you have an open mind as you've had all this while. Do you think you could manage that?"

"I guess I could," muttered Ezzy as he sank heavily into the leather sofa, his feigned restroom trip forgotten.

Toks began speaking softly as Soma nestled in beside her frowning husband. "You guys are parents so you'll be in the best position to relate with this analogy.

"Ezzy, imagine you've been away for a couple of weeks on a business trip. You're fatigued and can't wait to see your family again. And as you disembark and make your way out of the Arrival lounge, you see Soma and your two kids, what are their names?"

"Chidi and Bola," Soma replied.

"That's right. You see Chidi and Bola waiting for you and they're so excited, jumping all over you and hugging on you. So as you're all heading home, Chidi, as all kids do, then asks what you brought back for him from your trip.

"'Oh sorry son, I couldn't get you anything on this trip; maybe next time,' you rustle up an excuse.

"Chidi obviously isn't placated by your response so he begins to throw tantrums. So in order to calm him sufficiently, you reach into your wallet and bring out a hundred naira in ten naira bills; and as you know, little kids are less concerned about the value of the money than they are the number of the bills."

"That's true," Ezzy agreed, cracking a smile.

"So you count ten bills and hand them over to your son, who's now satisfied and content with his new found wealth. A few minutes later, you decide to test him to see whether he loves you more than the gift you just bestowed on him."

Ezzy squirmed. "I know where this is going," he groaned.

Toks ignored him and continued as Soma listened.

"So ever so casually, you ask Chidi to give you ten bucks, which is only 10% of the value of the money you so lovingly gave him. After some hesitation, Chidi reluctantly agrees; with the caveat that you'd return the money as soon as you get home. So you take his money and buy a breath mint, hearing Chidi again remind you that your debt must be paid."

"Hey, wait a sec!" Ezzy exclaimed mischievously. "Are you implying that I need a breath mint?"

"Maybe two." Toks replied sarcastically.

Soma and Toks laughed.

"As I was saying before I was interrupted, you're home now and trying to settle in. And no sooner are you out of the shower than your son's in your room, ready to collect."

"I no go woz am slap?" Ezzy growled, eliciting a smile from Toks.

"Why's that?" Toks asked. "He has a purely genuine reason to ask for what's his, doesn't he? After all, it's no longer complete. It's not a set of ten notes anymore. It's ten bucks short."

"No be me give am? Toks, bone that thing. I go woz am better slap!" Ezzy responded.

Soma leaned forward. It was all beginning to make sense.

Toks continued: "Now imagine Chidi's reaction when a day's passed and Daddy hasn't paid him back. Two days pass and still no word. Eventually, he decides to take matters into his own hands. He remembers that in Daddy's room, in the first shelf of his dresser drawer, his Dad often keeps loose change there--"

"Haaa! Na die be that now!" Ezzy exclaimed. "Pikin wey I born. Na im go come say he fit gboga me?"

Toks continued, ignoring Ezzy's tirade.

"--so in the middle of the night, just like a scene from *Mission Impossible,* he creeps in and makes his way stealthily across the floor. He gets to the dresser drawer, opens the shelf; and just as expected, he sees currency of different denominations; five naira, ten naira, fifty, hundred, two hundred, five hundred and one thousand naira notes strewn across it. He's not interested in the larger denominations, no, that's not why he's there. All he wants to do is to complete the set. All he needs is ten naira. He picks it up, stuffs it in his pajama pants, and creeps out the way he came, totally oblivious that his Dad had watched everything with one eye open.

"Now, as his father, how would you feel? Betrayed that your son didn't trust you enough to know you could give him more than the measly ten naira? Disappointed that he was a thief? Would you entrust more into his care? Now imagine this scene playing out every time you gave Chidi some money?"

"Toks, I go flog shege commot--" Ezzy froze as the message hit home.

"Gbam!" Soma exclaimed.

"I couldn't have said it better myself." Toks agreed as he sipped his glass of wine.

"A much better way to look at it would be remembering that tithing is an act of love, not a debt to be paid. I'll leave the theology to the preachers, but I decided a long time ago that what's 10% to the One who has given me everything? I mean, some folks would argue that tithing is an Old Testament idea and that Jesus only used it once in the New Testament"

"Yes na." Ezzy agreed. "I don check am sef. So if Jesus isn't making a big deal about it, why are the churches making it seem like you'll go to hell if you don't tithe. Guy, all na scam."

Toks shook his head. "I know it's an emotionally charged discussion, but I've come to realize that many people who are anti tithing feel that way because to be fair, churches aren't audited and aren't financially accountable to anyone. And they should be."

"You sef know," Ezzy concurred.

"But here's why I tithe, and trust me, I have to remind myself of this each time my income increases. I truly don't care if it's an Old Testament or New Testament argument. As you know, the word *testament,* is a legal word; and because it's so old school, let's replace it with the word, *Will.* So now, the Bible is divided into the Old Will and the New Will..."

"Sounds better to me," Soma said.

"Now, who writes the will?" Toks asked.

"I was gonna say something mischievous here, but I'm going to pass," Ezzy said, laughing. "You know what? I can't resist. Is the person that writes the will; the willer or the willee?"

"This man." Soma shook her head "What am I going to do with you?"

"Love me. Feed me, never leave me," Ezzy said, blowing her a kiss.

Toks continued.

"Let's just say the owner of the will, let's say the Father, in this case, God; wrote a Will. Now, who's the beneficiary of the will?"

"It would be his family."

"So I'm a beneficiary of His Will simply because I have a relationship with the owner."

"I see where you're going with this. It makes sense sha," Ezzy said, listening intently.

"So my point is, why argue whether it's the Old Will or the New Will, when I can be grateful that I'm even in His Will in the first place."

"That's deep," Soma said, scribbling.

"And if that doesn't float your boat, I've also heard some fellas use the analogy of insurance cover. So the tithe is like the monthly premium on your policy."

"Hmm. That makes a lot of sense," Ezzy concurred.

"Every time you pay, you're covered. So if something happens to you, your insurance provider is bound to compensate you for the damage incurred. Now, unlike most insurance companies, there isn't much red tape or bureaucracy involved. As long as you've tithed, if something falls through the cracks and you've incurred some level of damage, God is legally bound to compensate you. Now as you know, He doesn't ball in the minor leagues. So unlike the insurance companies that will return you to status quo, God is obligated to give you more than you lost, which is written boldly in His contract, and not in fine print."

"Omo, na to dey pay my monthly premium be dat before yawa come gas," Ezzy said, sipping his drink.

"Gbam!" Soma concurred a second time.

TOTAL MONEY WORKOUT

1. It's time to SIT your money. Draw up your plan

CHAPTER FIVE

MONEY TALKS

Secret 5: "Your values about money will determine your habits towards it."

Ezzy and Soma drove through the Lekki Admiralty Toll Plaza in silence, lost in thought as they pondered on the deeply profound thoughts Toks had shared.

As they made their way through the traffic on Ozumba Mbadiwe way, Soma finally spoke, "Omo man, Toks knows a heck of a lot of stuff! How did he get to be so well informed?"

"Well, I hear there's a cool new program that was invented not too long ago called the Internet," smirked Ezzy.

"Ezekiel Ayotunde! My husband, the practical joker," Soma retorted. "Perhaps you need to leave your day job and become a comedian, you're apparently quite good at it."

"Yeah right!" Ezzy scoffed.

"Babe but seriously, all the things Toks has shared with us from his Total Money Workout isn't found from Google oh. Do you think there's a correlation between Tokunbo's knowledge of money and its workings and his being financially secure?"

"I would think so, dear," Ezzy acquiesced. "All we've ever known about money has been either to work hard for it and how to spend it."

"Yeah, and look where it's gotten us," Soma agreed. "It's amazing to know how uncommon financial intelligence really is. I mean we go to school for years, acquire more degrees than thermometers, get good jobs and are clueless about making, managing and mastering money. No wonder so many seemingly successful people are poor."

"You can say that again."

They drove home in silence, each resolving to make better financial decisions.

WORK
11.27 am

"Amaka, did you hear the news?"

"Soma, leave me alone joor, I'm still not speaking to you."

"Amaka, I'm sorry, I know I deserve your silence, but this is important; and besides, this gist is fresh off the press."

Trying very hard to feign indifference, Amaka pried. "Oya, I'm listening and it had better be worth it."

Soma reached out and hugged Amaka.

"Let go, let go or you'll ruin my Zara suit!" Amaka laughed as she wriggled out of Soma's grip.

"You remember that bank that I wanted to joinl?" Soma asked.

"Yeah, Advantium Inc. What about them?" Amaka responded.

"They just laid off over 1300 people!"

"Jesus Christ!" Amaka cried. "That's so unfair, all those people. Kai! How will they cope? The country's hard enough the way it is, how do they expect them to manage?"

"My dear, I wish I had the answers to those questions," Soma said as she consoled her friend. "Sometimes, it's not until life slaps you on the face that you realize how close to falling off the edge you really are."

HOME
8:23pm

"Hey babe, how was work?" Ezzy asked as Soma flung herself onto the leather sofa.

"Dreadful," she muttered, rolling over to face her husband.

"No kidding! What happened?"

Soma recounted the day's events to Ezzy and watched as he heaved a huge sigh.

"Oh my. There's really no job security anymore, is there?" he asked.

"Seems so," Soma commiserated.

"It's almost like sitting on a three-legged stool and someone's trying to cut the legs from right under you," Ezzy continued.

"Only now, it seems that the number of stool cutters has increased exponentially and the number of stools has drastically reduced." Soma concurred. "Honey, I think we need to have another session with Toks again, don't you?"

"I do too, but I know he's incredibly busy at the moment. I'll call his cellphone and ask if we could schedule another appointment at his convenience," Ezzy said.

He chuckled. "We've turned Toks into our personal shrink."

"We're lucky we have him," Soma sighed.

"Imagine if those poor, unfortunate people who just lost their jobs had a Life Strategist like Toks guiding them; they would have been prepared to take whatever life threw at them, on their own terms."

CASA DE TOKS
2:00pm

"Hey bro, sorry to barge in again on you with our issues," apologized Ezzy.

"It's no bother at all," Toks responded. "I'll do what I can to make sure you both are financially fit and besides, I enjoy your company."

"But seriously, Toks, shouldn't we be paying you for this?" Soma asked.

"You should actually," Toks concurred. "And while I don't often say no to making money from my skills, I'll let this one be on the house."

"No Toks, we must," Soma insisted.

"Soma, don't force the issue. You heard the man," Ezzy drawled.

"I don't care what either of you say, but even if I can't pay for Toks' worth, I'm going to write a cheque in Toks' name."

With that, Soma reached into her handbag, rummaged for her cheque book and proceeded to write a cheque, which she then handed over to Toks, who seemed lost in thought.

"Toks, I know it's only a drop in the bucket compared to what you're worth, but it's just a token of my gratitude for sharing from the wells of wisdom that you carry. Would you please accept it from me?" Soma asked as she knelt in front of Toks.

"Please Soma, you don't have to kneel." Toks said, lifting her to her feet.

Ezzy couldn't help but wonder. What in the world is going on? Soma on her knees? For Tokunbo? The last time she ever went on her knees for me was at our traditional wedding ceremony.

Sensing Ezzy's discomfort, Toks pulled up a chair.

"Ezzy, my friend. Allow me to explain and ease your frayed nerves. In mastering wealth, there's a concept that most either ignore or are absolutely oblivious of."

"No kidding, I'm dying to know how kneeling is tied to making money." Ezzy scoffed as he glared at Soma.

Toks smiled.

"It's the law of sowing and reaping."

"That's it? That ain't new, I've heard about it a thousand times," Ezzy replied.

"I know you have, it states in simple fact that you cannot reap where you did not sow," Toks said.

"That doesn't count if you own the farm," Ezzy replied cheekily.

"Smart alec!" laughed Toks. "I do admire your ability to think outside the box.

"Most people don't ever recognize the principle that is sowing and reaping, because it's mostly perceived as spiritual. You have no right to take from a source when you are not connected to the source. Sure you can get marginal progress, but some things never get activated until you plug in. It's like being in a dark room. It's filled with latent electricity; but that power is useless to you until you connect your fan, or light bulb to the source."

"Makes sense," Ezzy agreed.

"Listen, man. Your seed is like a straw, it gives you the right to drink from the reservoir of blessing that the person carries. So not to sound spiritual or spooky, what your wife did was to gain access to what I carry, so don't take it personal." Toks smiled.

"Capisce?"

"Capisce, Godfather," Ezzy responded with a smile.

"Now that we've gotten that out of the way, what can I do for you guys?" Toks pressed the buzzer on his mahogany side stool. Immediately, a well-dressed butler walked into the living room.

"James, could we have some red wine? Would that be okay with you, Soma?"

"That's fine, thank you, Toks," Soma responded.

"Would that be all, sir?" the butler asked.

"Throw in some nuts too, would you?"

"Very well, sir." James walked off to get their order.

"I've got to get me one of those, man," Ezzy remarked, looking at the butler walking away.

"All in good time, my friend. Let's get your money out of the woods first." Toks smiled.

The butler returned with their drinks and nuts. "Thank you James. That will be all."

"Very well, sir," the butler nodded as he left the room.

"Seriously man, I gotta get me one of these butlers." Ezzy grinned.

"I must warn you, they cost more than a pretty penny and you know you're pretty short of pennies." Toks retorted.

"Touché! Nice one. You got me right below the belt," Ezzy doubled over, in mock pain.

"You guys are just big kids refusing to grow up," Soma smiled.

"Perhaps, but we have bigger toys now," Ezzy laughed.

"Oya Toks, please we have bigger fish to fry. I'm very worried," Soma fretted.

"What's wrong?"

"Did you hear of the recent layoffs in the Banking sector?" Soma asked.

"I did. Quite a number of people I know were affected. I hear they went to work and just couldn't log in to their system and that was it. Very sad." Toks replied.

"I'm particularly worried because you know, I'm a banker. I'm scared that I could go to work one day and find out I'm out of a job." Soma said as sobs began to rack her slender frame.

Ezzy put his arms around his wife and comforted her as Toks brought a box of tissues.

"Don't worry, dear, that's not going to happen," Ezzy whispered as he dabbed Soma's eyes with the tissues.

"But it could," Toks replied.

"God forbid!" Ezzy countered. "Toks, how could you be so insensitive?"

"Relax, bro. I'm not suggesting that Soma would get fired, far from it. It however is a vague possibility and I need her to live as though she could lose her job tomorrow."

"Where's the fun in that? Besides, isn't that going to make her live in fear?" Ezzy retorted.

"Not when placed in the proper perspective. It'll just make her more aware of her buying and spending decisions. If it wasn't that important to me, you wouldn't be on this Total Money Workout programme."

"Listen fellas, we're on the same side. You've learned a lot over the last couple of weeks and I think you're doing great, which is more than I can say for those poor unfortunate souls who don't understand how their money talks."

"Money talks? I only hear mine when I go to retrieve cash from the ATM and she says the same thing all the time: you have insufficient funds in your account." Ezzy laughed.

“No more insufficient funds!” Soma sang.

"Here's hoping our Able God can change that," Toks smiled.

"Toks, could you explain how our money talks?” Soma asked as she dried her eyes.

"I will, only if you start smiling," Toks responded.

"Done!" Soma smiled as she blew her nose and passed Ezzy the tissue.

"Gross," moaned Ezzy as he stuffed the used tissue into his jacket.

Toks began.

"Money talks, but you've got to learn the language. Your values towards money will determine your habits towards it. Every single person has what I call a money personality. Your money personality is the way you have learned to treat and respond to the acquisition and disbursement of money. Your money personality affects your financial decision making styles."

"Sounds complicated," muttered Ezzy.

"Nothing you can't handle, I assure you." Toks smiled as he continued. “Are you with me so far, Soma?"

"Aye Aye, Captain," Soma said with mock salute.

"Ezzy, think of your money personality as a language, say French and Soma, let's say yours is Mandarin. If I were to lock you up for a day and expect you to communicate, how well would you fare?"

"Pretty poorly, I'm sure," Ezzy replied.

"Xue guoyu bu tai nan," Toks answered.

"Say what, say what, say what? Toks, did you just speak Chinese?"

Toks laughed heartily. "That's one of the perks of being an international businessman. Allow me to translate. All I said was, 'it's not too hard to learn Mandarin'."

"Bros, you lost me there."

"My point exactly. That's what happens when two people who have different money personalities are expected to agree on how to manage it. They'll definitely have conflicts because of the way their money talks."

"Deep stuff, bro. So now you've got me. What are the types of money personalities that people have and how do we manage them?"

"I'm glad you asked. There are four basic types of money personality and each person often has a primary and secondary money personality. So you are either The Saver, The ATM or Debit Card, The Vault or The Hole."

"I definitely know which one I am. The Big, Black Hole," Ezzy said ruefully.

"It's okay, honey. I'm sure I'm the ATM," Soma replied.

"Toks, while the names are easy enough to determine what category one falls into, could you define them individually?" Soma asked.

"Sure thing," Toks replied.

"The Saver, as the name implies, is more concerned with saving money and having short term security. He dreads having little or nothing in his bank accounts as he often equates his financial statement with his life's value. He could be disciplined or pretty frugal when it comes to spending, but is more inclined to have little nest eggs stowed away for the rainy day."

"Nest egg? Poach the eggs, I don't even have a nest!"

"That's why we're on this path, bro. Personal finance is 80% behavior and 20% knowledge. So if I can give you some knowledge and change your behavior, the rest, they say, is history."

"I'll be history if I don't get my act together," Ezzy smirked.

"Let's move on to the next one." Toks poured Ezzy a drink as he continued, "Let's talk about the ATM."

"I'm sure you're talking about me right now," Soma smiled. "Go ahead, Toks, hit me! I can take it."

Toks laughed heartily and reached for the peanuts. "I'm glad one of us is looking at the bright side of things," he remarked with a sly grin at Ezzy.

"So, while the Saver is concerned about saving money for the rainy day, the ATM money personality is most and generally concerned with living on the sunny side of life; and as you can imagine, the ATM is a spender. This person lives by Drake'sYOLO philosophy."

"YOLO? What's that?" Soma asked.

Ezzy got off his seat and cheered, "Dude, I didn't know you were feeling Young Money! Young Moolah, baby!" The two men high-fived.

"Huh? YOLO? Young Money? You guys have me confused," Soma complained, arms flailing in the air.

"Sorry babe. YOLO is an acronym for You Only Live Once and Young Money is a record label that Drake's signed to," Ezzy explained.

"I get it now. For a moment, I thought you guys were trying to keep me in the dark," Soma replied.

"As I was saying, the ATM's spending philosophy is you only live once and he really lives it up. Every bonus or cash gift is treated with the initial thought of 'what can I buy with this?'The lack of cash is not a deterrent to the ATM who believes he can always write post-dated cheques to meet a need for instant gratification."

"Oooohhhhh!" Soma grimaced covering her eyes with her palm. "That is so me. I'm so embarrassed."

"There's nothing to be ashamed of Soma, most people fall into this category." Toks replied.

"Yeah, babes, you're in good company," Ezzy smiled as he hugged his wife. "Unless of course you want to trade places with the Hole."

"Nooooooo!" Soma shrieked. "I'll take my chances with being the ATM.

"But seriously, Toks, is there a problem with spending money once I have it?" Soma asked.

"Not at all," Toks replied. "We need to spend money. It drives the wheels of trade and economy. But the difference between the Saver and the ATM is the priority they place on what they do with the money. You see, the Saver saves first and spends what's left over; but the ATM spends first and then saves whatever's left over, if there's anything left over."

"I get it now!" Soma exclaimed.

"Don't forget that Toks said your money personality can be a blend of two or more personalities, you'll just have one that is more predominant than the others," Ezzy added.

"Attaboy Ezzy! It's good to know that you actually understand this." Toks smiled at his mischievous friend.

"Don't get it twisted, Toks, I'm smart and not just a pretty face," Ezzy replied cheekily.

"I won't," smiled Toks. "And besides, you're not a pretty face."

"Tell us about the Vault, Toks," Soma pleaded.

"Sure thing, Soma. The Vault, as the name implies, is a financial storehouse. He believes in building and replicating his investments. He's not one of those fickle short-term investors, who are just investing to make a quick buck; no sir, he's in it for the long haul. The Vault has a huge asset portfolio that he's constantly building--"

"He sounds boring. I hate him already," Ezzy interrupted. "So all he does is gather money, sit and count his millions all day? Where's the fun in that?"

Toks laughed heartily.

"Of course not. He simply understands and implements the secrets of wealth that I've been sharing with you. He's not some Ebenezer Scrooge who's just hoarding money and being stingy. The Vault realizes that he's a custodian of wealth and has built great mental and material capacity to handle money. So unlike the ATM and the Hole, he's not a subject to money; here, the roles are reversed, money works for him."

"Okay, nuff said. I'm dying to know about the big, black Hole. I'm sure he's a lot more fun," Ezzy chuckled.

"Absolutely!" Toks concurred. "He totally swallows you up, if you know what I mean. The Hole is perhaps the least financially savvy and least disciplined of all the money personalities. He's also very generous and charitable. He's pretty much driven by 100% impulse, both to give and to spend. For him, there's always a plan, a scheme or an angle he's working, hoping that this one would be his big break. When it comes to making financial decisions, he pretty much plays it by ear."

"Sounds like someone I know," Soma said, grinning at her husband.

"Sounds like a fun guy. Definitely someone I'd share a beer with," smirked Ezzy.

"Buying drinks is what helped create the hole in the first place," Toks countered, laughing.

"You've got a point there," Ezzy conceded.

He reached for his now empty wine glass and proceeded to refill it. "Wine, the ambrosia of the gods," he muttered before taking a sip from his glass. Soma shook her head disapprovingly.

"Toks, is there a more scientific way to prove what our money personalities are?" Soma asked.

"Most definitely, Soma. I think I have a Total Money Workout money personality assessment somewhere in my study," Toks replied as he rose. "I'll be right back."

"He's definitely making a lot of sense," Ezzy remarked. "Toks no be money miss road."

"At all o!" Soma concurred.

"Our sessions with Toks have taught me that while it requires a particular set of skills to make money, it requires a different skillset and much greater discipline to keep and multiply it." Ezzy said.

"You can say that again," Soma readily agreed.

"Found it." Toks strode into the living room with a wide grin. "Now let's see how your money talks."

TOTAL MONEY WORKOUT

1. What's your money personality?

CHAPTER SIX

YOUR MONEY MENTALITY

Secret 6: "Your money has got a mind of its own and its future decisions are determined by its past experiences"

CASA DE TOKS

"Toks, I'm telling you, man, this stuff is hard," Ezzy moaned.

"Nothing good comes easy, bro. If you want to get a six pack, you're going to have to cut out the junk food and start doing those crunches. Not fun at all. The same rules apply to having a Total Money Workout," Toks replied.

"So you mean I can't buy stuff and pay later? I have access to some credit from my bank that will foot this bill easily. All I need to do is spread the payment over a period of three to six months."

"I think you know my answer by now," Toks said with a grin.

They had walked into the Samsung store to look at the latest gadgets and Ezzy hadn't been able to take his eyes off the Samsung QLED TV.

"Jeez!" He exclaimed. "Would you look at that sexy looking work of Asian goodness? Get thee behind me, Samsung."

"Too late," Toks replied. "It's right in front of you."

"I have the perfect wall for the perfect TV." Ezzy stepped forward, taking a closer look. "And this TV is effin' perfect!" he concluded.

"Breathe, man, breathe. Back away from the device. Walk towards the light." Toks was grinning as he pulled his friend out of the store.

"Ooooohhh! Toks. This ain't fair, man. I've been on this Total Money Workout diet for a long time now. I'm getting bored jare. Even athletes have cheat days."

"Agreed, but it takes one splurge on the wrong cheat day to get you back in the habit of craving the junk food that you've so painstakingly fought against," Toks continued. "Listen man, you're doing great so far and yes, I agree that you might need to reward yourself for your consistency, but let's think for a moment, shall we?"

"Ooooooh, Toks. I know you're gonna give me a lecture right now, but I'm really not in the mood for one."

"Fair enough," Toks retorted. "But let me ask you this, were you thinking about owning this TV before we got here?"

"Err...not exactly, but--"

"Don't butt in at the moment and yes, pun intended. So would I be right to assume that this right here is an impulsive decision?"

"Well..." Ezzy muttered under his breath.

"Sorry, I didn't quite hear you. I'm going to need you to speak up a bit." Toks smiled. He had his old friend cornered and he wasn't about to let up so easily.

"Yeah, okay, okay," Ezzy surrendered. "So it's an impulsive decision, but you can't blame me. But did you see the size of that thing?"

"Yeah I did, and you'd be paying for it, long after the excitement of the purchase has worn off and trust me, the pain of paying debt is way heavier than the cost of acquiring it; and besides, it's not smart to finance liabilities with a liability. No, scratch that last part; allow me rephrase it. It's pretty dumb to finance liabilities with a liability."

"Hmm...It's pretty dumb to finance liabilities with a liability." Ezzy repeated the words aloud. "It all makes sense, Toks. I know it feels good spending and it feels bad paying it back, but I still don't feel better about not getting this TV."

"Truth is, you won't," Toks empathized with him. "But what we can do is for you to reward yourself with this TV after you've disciplined your money. Let's get some ice cream and I'll explain; by the way, you're buying."

"No way, my Life Strategist insists that I need to discipline my money," Ezzy laughed.

"Cheapskate," Toks shot back. "But weren't you about to pay for a big ass TV?"

"That's how I roll. I ball big and don't play in the minor leagues." Toks grinned as he pulled up a chair at the Coldstone Creamery. As they placed their orders, he noticed Toks listening intently to a news anchor on the cable television talking about the plight of starving children in Africa.

"Dude, what's with the Jedi concentration?" Ezzy asked.

"Sorry, man, I was just caught up with how the Western media love to show Africa as a habitat with malnourished children, drinking dirty water and the likes," Toks fumed.

"It ticks me off too," Ezzy agreed.

"But you know what?"

"What?"

"I couldn't help but see beyond the obvious."

"See beyond the obvious? You've lost me," Ezzy said as he took a scoop of his ice cream sundae.

"I was looking at these malnourished children and I couldn't help but notice the parallels between nutrition and financial fitness," Toks explained.

"Parallels?" Ezzy asked, through a mouthful of his ice cream.

"I'm thinking there are three levels of financial fitness," Toks replied digging in.

"Go on," Ezzy coerced.

"The first financial fitness status is the malnourished state or malnourished money. Here, you're barely making enough money to sustain you. You aren't getting the necessary financial nutrients you need to make a living.

“Here, your basic need is for survival; looking for the next paycheck. Here, you're not particularly worried about having more assets than liabilities, everything around you seems like a liability," Toks said.

"That's true, bro," Ezzy replied. "Sounds pretty rough. But how does one get out of this state?”

"Well, like I've said before, wealth is first, a state of mind. You've got to get your money mentality right," Toks replied.

"Bros, you don come o. Which one be money mentality again?" Ezzy quipped.

Toks laughed. "Your money mentality refers to the limiting or empowering belief systems you have concerning money, particularly the acquisition and distribution of it."

"Sounds complicated." Ezzy stared ruefully at his half empty ice cream cup.

"Not a bit. Let me explain," Toks said as he pulled his chair closer. "Your life experiences determine your belief systems. Your belief systems determine your decisions and those decisions will determine your destiny."

"Yep, that's what I said, complicated," Ezzy chuckled.

Toks grinned as he continued.

"We are all a function of our environment, the constant battle between nature and nurture. Let me break it down. I was raised in a less than middle class family. My parents were civil servants and were constantly trying to climb their career ladder, their reasoning was simple: The higher you climbed, the more money you made. So life was a constant struggle for my parents, because they were truly stuck in the proverbial rat race with lots of motion and no movement. Life for my parents was a series of battles between pay checks and bills, eventually having more bills than money. It was a pretty hard life. When I'd ask my dad for money, I'd get the usual rebuttal 'do you think money grows on trees?' or my personal favorite, 'don't you know we're managing?'"

Ezzy chuckled, "I thought it was only my popsie that used to say that."

Toks grinned. "That makes two of us. So being raised in that kind of environment created my money mentality, which could be summarized as: money must be toiled for to be acquired and stingily managed to be retained."

"Hmm...that's deep," Ezzy replied. "I think my money mentality can be summarized by: money no dey come fast, but money quick dey go, so make I spend am sharply before breeze blow am go."

"Exactly! So you see that our life experiences with money have created our belief systems or money mentality," Toks said emphatically.

"Chai!" Ezzy exclaimed from the profundity of Toks' analysis and also from realizing that his ice cream was finished. Disheartened, he asked, "so how do I change my money mentality?"

"Create a new belief system," Toks replied. "Here's how I changed mine. So after I'd been married for about 2 years, I developed the habit of taking my family out for lunch after church on Sundays, simply because my wife kept complaining about how unromantic and cheap I was, preferring to eat home-cooked meals than to go out to eat at a nice place, which was predicated by another money mentality – spending money equates to wasting money."

"Guy, I know that move. I used to tell Soma that I wanted to eat her delicious cooking because I didn't want to spend money."

"Abi o!" Toks replied. "My wife would make sure she ordered something expensive and man, when the bill would come, I'd find my heart racing at a thousand beats per minute and after paying, I'd be irritable and cranky because as far as I was concerned, virtue had left me; which leads me to my next thought about having a money mentality; what emotion do you experience when you have to spend money?"

"Hmm...deep. What emotion do you experience when you have to spend money?" Ezzy muttered.

Toks continued.

"For me, my constant emotions were sadness, anxiety and anger. My money mentality towards eating out at fancy restaurants was, people like me don't deserve to be in places like this."

"Wow!" exclaimed Ezzy. "People like me don't deserve to be in places like this. That's deep, bro."

Toks agreed, "Yeah, I always felt like I was a slave to money, the acquisition of it made me feel good and the attendant loss of it always made me feel bad. I knew something had to give. I needed to change."

"True that, bro," Ezzy concurred. "So what did you do?"

"You wouldn't believe it," Toks grinned.

"Try me," Ezzy smiled.

"So I recognized that these money mentalities were a huge limiting belief or mental block and I needed to change the program that I was running. So one day, I decided to drive into the Eko Hotels & Suites by myself."

"For real?" Ezzy asked.

"For real, bro. I decided to run a test pilot. I didn't take my family with me just in case I took them in and couldn't afford to bring them out."

Ezzy couldn't help laughing and neither could Toks.

"I know the feeling," Ezzy choked through his tears. "Man, this stuff is real."

"Check it out: So as I drove in, I noticed there was a security barrier where we needed to punch in to get a ticket. So as I did the needful, I noticed there was a sign right beside the barrier."

"What did it say?" Ezzy asked.

"It said parking for the first fifteen minutes was free, but every hour after that would attract a two hundred naira fee."

"Makes sense" Ezzy remarked.

"Perhaps," Toks agreed. "But remember that this was many years ago and because of my programming and attendant limiting beliefs, I remember thinking that I wouldn't be there longer than fifteen minutes, and subsequently setting a timer on my phone."

"No way, man!" Ezzy couldn't help laughing. Interestingly, listening to Toks share his experiences made his seemingly larger-than-life friend seem a lot more human.

"So now I am on the clock," Toks continued, "I quickly drive in and find a parking spot. I'm not familiar with the surroundings and also don't want to ask for directions; don't want anyone knowing it's my first time. Lost a few minutes finding my way, but eventually locate the restaurant, pull up a chair and hey presto! The waiter shows up with two menus."

"I shudder to think of what happened next," Ezzy interjected.

"Allow me to put you out of your misery," Toks replied. "So he hands me the menu. I'm solely focused on the drinks menu, because as far as I'm concerned, I can tell how much the food will cost by how much the drinks cost."

"Word! I'll drink to that," Ezzy said as he raised his glass.

"I open the menu, looking as cool as a cucumber on the outside, but raging like a storm in a teacup on the inside. I don't know if you've ever done this before, something I call, shopping on the right side of the menu?"

"Dude, I thought I was the only one that did that!" Ezzy exclaimed spilling his drink.

They laughed.

"Don't we all?!" Toks slapped Ezzy on the back as he began a coughing spell. "Guy, easy dey laugh o, no use laugh come die."

He continued.

"After looking at the price list instead of the item, I ordered a Coke which coincidentally, was the cheapest drink on the menu at a thousand naira. A few minutes later, he returns with my drink; a glass of Coca Cola filled with ice and a slice of lemon and cucumber."

"The good life!" Ezzy toasted.

"Yeah, so I've heard," Toks scoffed. "Anyway, so he brings the drink and pours the Coke into the glass. Once the glass is full and the bottle is half empty, he does the unthinkable--"

"What did he do?" Ezzy asked with eyes wide open.

"He takes the bottle away!"

"Nooooooo!" Ezzy yelled, immediately relapsing into another coughing fit.

"As you can imagine, I'm not used to this kind of behavior, based on my life experience, so I call him back to return my half full bottle."

"You. Did. Not!" Ezzy spelt out in shock.

"Of course I did, that's where my money mentality kicked in. I said, dude, do you know how many bottles of Coca Cola you can buy with a thousand bucks? That's about half of a crate! I just paid a thousand bucks for a single bottle, so I'm gonna drink every drop."

"As in!" Ezzy concurred, laughing.

Toks continued, wiping a tear from his eye.

"The waiter returns the bottle and with a cheeky grin on his face, says to me,it's your first time, abi?"

With that, Ezzy immediately burst into another laughing and coughing fit.

"I honestly can't believe that you went through all of that, Toks," Ezzy said after he regained his composure. "I mean I look at you today, all poised and confident, got-it-going-on, and I can't relate it to the fella you described. They sound like two different people."

"I know man. You know what it says in Scripture, as a man thinks in his heart or mind, so is he. So once my money mentality changed, my habits followed, my life changed."

"True that," Ezzy concurred. "But I remember you saying there were three levels of financial fitness. What's the next one?"

"Let's think it through this way. So imagine we've kept the malnourished level at bay and we're on a weight loss or fitness program, we're going to work our way down the two remaining levels: overweight and healthy."

"Sounds like a plan."

"Okay. So the second level of financial fitness is being financially overweight or obese," Toks began.

"I don't see how that's a bad thing," Ezzy disagreed. "Doesn't it mean that my money is so stacked that it's put on some pounds?"

"Nice double entendre," Toks grinned. "Great word play. But it's not the same thing."

"Oya explain," Ezzy said. "But this explanation had better be good, cause one blogger chic just bought a crib on the Island for over half a billion naira and you're telling me that her money ain't stacked or blown up. Lord, blow me up, blow my money up!"

Toks laughed heartily and wiped his tears. He hadn't laughed this hard in a while; coaching Ezzy and Soma was as good for him as it was for them.

"Nah, her money ain't overweight," he said, "it's pretty healthy, but I'll get to that in a bit, so stay with me."

"The second level of financial fitness is fat money or when your finances are overweight. As you know, being overweight simply suggests that you're taking in more than what you're burning. So when your money is overweight, while you're making money, you're spending way more than you're making, just eating through your income so quickly that you have more liabilities than assets".

"Hmmm..." Ezzy muttered under his breath. "Sounds interesting and very familiar."

"Yeah," Toks concurred. "So the weight isn't from the volume of the income, but from the volume of the liabilities and debt. So the extra pounds ain't more dollars, it's more debt. And the attendant weight or debt eventually piles up, one pound at a time, slowing down your productivity, until previously simple tasks that you once took for granted become hard and next to impossible until your debt profile eventually becomes a mass of deadweight. All because you refused to put your finances on a strict financial fitness regimen."

"Daaaammmnnnn!" exclaimed Ezzy. "Toks, this is insane! You've just told me the story of my life in one paragraph."

Toks grinned. "That's what I do, bro, I give wake up calls. And you just got yours."

"Tell me about it, man," Ezzy said as he wiped his brow. "Man, Toks, for real though, I can't thank you enough for how you've helped Soma and I become financially fit over the last couple of months. Just having you as our Life Strategist has not only improved our finances, but in a weird way, it's drastically improved our marriage. We argue less, I seem to make fewer mistakes in Soma's eyes, though I ain't sure I've changed much; she's less of a drama queen and we're more of a team than we've been over the last couple of years."

Toks shrugged it off. "I didn't do a thing, man. You were humble and honest enough to realize that you needed help and you had the guts to ask for it. Unfortunately, most people are in denial, or just think that the Nile is only a river in Egypt--"

"Haaaaaaa! Nice one, man!" Ezzy cheered. "I see what you did there. Nice word play. Denial – the Nile, bad guy!"

"I give as good as I get. Thought for a minute that it'd sail right over you, but this is proof positive that you don't have a bag of marbles in your cranium," Toks countered. "But seriously, though, most people are in denial. They don't believe they have a problem. They seem to have the trappings of success, but don't realize they've been trapped by success."

"Word! They seem to have the trappings of success, but don't realize they've been trapped by success." Ezzy muttered.

"Absolutely. They don't realize that everything in life is connected. It's like a spider web, each thread's connected; pull one off and the delicate balance is affected. Once your money starts acting funny, it affects your psychology, which in turn, affects your health, which invariably affects your relationships and throws your life out of whack and the same goes for other dimensions of your life."

"That's some deep stuff," Ezzy concurred. Pausing to think, he asked, "So what about the third financial fitness status? Healthy money?"

"Well," Toks began. "It's pretty self-explanatory. But the basic idea behind having healthy money is that you're making more than enough to meet and cover your needs. You have a low debt-to-income ratio, or simply put, your assets far outweigh your debt."

"You're definitely not a selfie holder or investor," Ezzy remarked.

"Definitely not," Toks concurred. "Here, you've definitely created a system that not only creates wealth for you, but manages and multiplies it absolutely devoid of your personal effort and involvement.

"So just like any good workout, keep your money on the right fitness regimen.

Give your money a good workout. It might be painful at the start, but if you're consistent and don't have too many cheat days, you'll love the results at the end."

CASA DE TOKS

"But Toks, hold on oh. There's something that has been bothering me," Ezzy said, looking worried. He and Soma were at Toks' again, already deep into another Total Money Workout session.

"I'm all ears," Toks replied. "What's up?"

"It seems a bit weird to explain, but it's like no matter what I do, I can't earn beyond a certain amount of money. For example, with my salary and even side hustles, I can't seem to hit one million Naira in a month. I mean, I fit do N500k, sometimes maybe N700k, but I no fit hit 1M. E be like say my village people day do me."

"That one sef dey," Toks said laughing.

"But seriously bro. That means you've hit your money ceiling."

"Money ceiling?" Soma asked. "I didn't know it was possible to hit a ceiling in your finances."

"Oh yes it is and what Ezzy has described is absolutely accurate, though most people are oblivious to it."

"Count me in," Soma concurred. "I didn't know anything about this until you mentioned this."

"Okay, let's make this actionable. Think about an amount of money that you feel absolutely comfortable generating as income on a monthly basis."

"Should it be what I currently earn?" Soma asked.

"Not necessarily. Just an amount of money you feel comfortable generating."

"Okay nah, let's go there. I don write 2 milla." Ezzy grinned, typing the number into his phone.

"Whatever floats your boat bro, but whatever you write first shouldn't shake you."

"Me, I'm sha writing N600k. I cannot come and kill myself," Soma replied.

"Oya make I respect myself, I don write 1M." Ezzy grinned.

Toks continued.

"Now, double that number."

"That's 1.2 million naira," Soma said, "Omo!"

"Mine is 2 million bucks as a bad guy."

"Now double it," Toks said.

"Haaa. Toks, is this money per month or per year?" Soma asked.

"Omo, this is almost my annual salary," Ezzy said, shaking his head.

"Okay, let's go one step forward. I'd like you to double that figure."

"Ah ahhh," Ezzy exclaimed,"Na jazz? Is all this money coming from my salary or maybe from some unexpected long lost relative who put me in his will?"

"Should I keep doubling?" Toks asked

"Noooo!" Soma and Ezzy both yelled in unison.

"And that, my dear friends, is your money ceiling," Toks said, smiling. "Let me ask a few questions and I need you to be completely honest with me."

"Absolutely Toks," Soma replied.

"At what number did you start getting uncomfortable?" Toks asked.

"To be honest man, it was from the first number. I know I said 2 million bucks from the beginning, but I didn't even believe it. Even the N1 million that I said sef, my heart no fit carry am. Na my mouth talk am, e no reach my heart," Ezzy responded.

"That's deep, bro and exactly why most people plateau. Their hearts are not in sync with what their mouths say."

"I actually wrote N800k, cancelled it and then wrote N600k, which is slightly double my present salary. I kept asking myself if I was going to use jazz to make that money," Soma concurred.

"And the interesting thing is that your subconscious mind records and documents this behavior. Remember I said previously that why we plateau is because our hearts are not in sync with what our mouths say. Have you ever wanted to buy a particular car and all of a sudden, you start seeing the car everywhere?"

"Yes oh! It's almost like they're mass producing it." Soma laughed.

"And as you know, it's not being mass produced. Your subconscious mind has only recognized there's a sync between your heart and mind as has now brought what you desire into focus."

"30 billion fall on me," Ezzy said, laughing. "I don blow."

"Unfortunately, it doesn't exactly work that way, bro. One of the roles of the subconscious mind is to keep you safe and keep you the same. Based on your life experiences, your subconscious creates a self image of who you truly are. Think of it like DNA, which defines a genetic code into your system. So anything that doesn't reflect or align with your self image is filtered away from you."

"My village people oh!" Soma said.

"I know right?" Toks grinned. "Think about it this way, whenever there's an earthquake, its seismic activity is registered on a Richter scale; and in the same vein, every emotional response is measured in your mind's Richter scale. Now, when you say 30 billion fall on me or Dangote money fall on me, your subconscious scans for emotional responses. Every negative response reminds your mind of fear and once it finds it, do you remember what one of the roles of the subconscious is?"

"To keep you safe and keep you the same," Soma read from her notes.

"Exactly, so your mind registers your fear as perceived danger and unfortunately, because it can't tell the difference between real or perceived danger, it lumps it all as a threat to its continued survival and because it doesn't align with your self image, it filters it away and keeps you safe by getting rid of that threat."

"My village people getting rid of my destiny oh!" Soma screamed again.

Toks couldn't help laughing.

"Let's bring it back to your money ceiling. So the moment your subconscious detects fear in your heart because of the amount of money you mentioned, let's say 30 billion, it realizes that amount of money is way above your self image, and so it places a ceiling on the amount you last felt comfortable, which was how much?"

"Less than a million," Ezzy said ruefully.

"N600k," Soma said biting her pen.

"So right now, your subconscious mind believes that it's not safe for Soma to earn more than N600k at any given time and so, it will sabotage every opportunity for her to earn more because it doesn't reflect with her self image," Toks continued.

"I bind it in Jesus name. The devil is a liar!" Soma said, snapping her fingers around her head.

"Unfortunately, this particular devil doesn't go away by binding and loosing."

"This just got real, bro. I mean, I just realized that I always talk myself out of opportunities to earn more. I keep saying shit like it'll be too much work, or I don't have the right connections and somehow somehow, I just blow it off and fashy the chance to make more, even if my mouth talks a big game," Ezzy said.

"That's your subconscious sabotaging you right there."

"So how do we reprogram our subconscious minds?" Soma asked, quite worried.

"It's all about exposure. Like I said, your subconscious doesn't know the difference between facts and fiction. It can't tell the difference between your personal experiences and those of others, nor the difference between dreams and reality. That's why you can dream intensely and it all feels so real and wake up in a cold sweat."

"Man, I had a dream that Soma's village people were chasing me." Ezzy laughed.

"That's because you haven't finished paying bride price na," Soma responded cheekily.

"Shots fired!" Toks smiled as Soma hit her husband with a pillow. He continued, "like I was saying, your subconscious can't tell the difference between your personal experiences and those of others."

"Come oh. Toks. Does that mean I should be like that blogger that went to pose in front of some rich guy's 7 bedroom mansion and now claimed she had built it for her birthday so she could tension people on the Gram?" Soma asked.

"For real?" Toks said shocked.

"Yes oh! Until Instablog busted her and she now admitted it was a lie."

"No, that's simply being deceitful." Toks replied, waving it aside.

"Maybe she's claiming it by faith or using it as a point of contact?" Ezzy smirked.

"Nah, the aim is obviously to manipulate. Listen guys, I know there are a lot of funny people out there who, like Soma said, are trying to tension people on the Gram, but that's not what I mean. You have to deliberately bypass your subconscious."

"Sounds sneaky," Soma said, rubbing her hands gleefully. "Like something out of the Mission Impossible movies."

Toks continued.

"Your subconscious can't decipher a real experience from an imaginary one. So for example, you may never have travelled abroad before, but you can dream you're out of the country..."

"Man, like I've been dreaming that I've been in Canada since," Ezzy said wistfully.

"You and who? I'm sha not going with you," Soma said, playfully shoving her husband.

Toks smiled and continued."You better wake up. But seriously, have you ever been to Canada?"

"Only in my dreams," Ezzy remarked.

"But how do you know that's where you were?" Toks asked.

"I don't know, but I sha know that was Canada because of all the snow and plenty Oyinbo people."

"So what you're saying is you recognize a place you've never been?"

"Err, something like that," Ezzy said, scratching his head.

"Exactly!" Toks said, rubbing his hands excitedly. "Your subconscious mind saved images of places and possibly, people in Canada and superimposed you there, even without you ever setting foot there. The language of the subconscious is pictures and imagery while the language of the conscious mind is logic. Think of it this way. Your subconscious mind is like how you use the Instagram app. You keep scrolling the timeline, looking at pictures; and once you find one you resonate with, you like it. But that's not all, you actually save the pictures that you have a strong emotional connection to, whether they're positive or negative."

"So your self image is like a collection of saved Instagram pictures," Soma said.

"Exactly!" Toks said "You can like pictures from morning till night, but what the subconscious really focuses on are the pictures you save."

"So the subconscious builds your self image from the negative responses you've saved," Soma clarified.

"Absolutely. So just like your Instagram app, it notices the posts you've saved and the algorithm automatically starts showing you more of those kind of posts in your explore page. So in the same vein, your subconscious shows you more of the experiences you've saved. So imagine having different picture collections or folders on Money & Finance, Love & Relationships, Business & Career and so on."

"Flipping scary, man," Ezzy said. "So how does this help break my money ceiling?"

"Like I said, you've got to bypass your subconscious. That's why some people use vision boards, where they put pictures of what they desire, especially in a location they'll see it the most..."

"Like the bathroom mirror," Soma interjected.

"Absolutely. Your subconscious is aware of its surroundings, even if you're not conscious of what's around you. This causes the subconscious to store those images in its saved folder. Next and perhaps the most important thing you can do to raise your money ceiling is by being exposed to people whose floors are higher than your ceilings."

"Tweetable!" Soma yelled, scribbling into her trusty notebook.

"Damn! Being exposed to people whose floors are higher than your ceilings. Sounds like you're talking about yourself right now," Ezzy smirked.

"Well, people like me and to be clear, I'm not talking about some money-miss-road individual who probably inflated government contracts and is now living on Easy Street. You'll only expose yourself to getting the wrong values. I'm talking about learning how to build wealth, and particularly seeing how wealthy business people think."

"Me, I've seen how you think, Toks and all I can say is that I've got a long way to go," Soma said, picking up some nuts from the serving tray before them.

"We sure do," Ezzy concurred emptying his glass.

TOTAL MONEY WORKOUT

1. What's your money mentality?
2. What are your limiting beliefs about money? Don't be embarrassed. Write them all down.
3. What 5 empowering beliefs can you create about money?
4. What's your money ceiling? Be honest. At what number did you get uncomfortable?
5. What 5 things could you do now to break your money ceiling?

CHAPTER SEVEN

POOR MONEY

Secret 7: "You can't help the poor if you're one of them.
The greater the poverty weight you carry, the poorer you become"

LUNCH ROOM

"Don Ezzy, where've you been, man? Haven't seen you at The Lounge in ages," Hassan said as he hugged his friend.

"Just been busy, bruv. Trying to get my act together." Ezzy replied.

"No kidding, man? I know the feeling. Abeg, can you hook a brotha up, cause I'm broke and need to make this paper."

"Haba Hassan, you can't be serious. We got our paycheck last week. There ain't no way you could've blown all that money that soon; abi you dey build house and you no wan tell me ba?"

"Which kain house? Na spit dem dey take make block? Guy, leave that matter, abeg loan me some cash to tide me over till our next paycheck."

"Dude," Ezzy replied. "Turn me upside down and shake me inside out, me sef no get shishi."

"Damn!" Hassan hissed. "It's been one of those months. I'm stressed out. Had to sort out some stuff for my in-laws, pay my kids' school fees cause they resumed last week, and then I had to pay off some outstanding loans that my Popsy has. It's eaten up all my income for the month and more."

"That's rough," Ezzy said, putting his hand on Hassan's shoulder.

"Dude, you don't know the half of it," Hassan continued. "I'm stressed, man. It's bad enough that what I make is barely enough to keep me afloat, but when I consider all the dependents I have, I feel like I'm just working for them."

Ezzy could understand.

"I feel your pain, bruv. When you have dependents, you can depend on them to leave dents in your finances. I don't know what it is, but I also think it's pretty unfair. Our folks, God bless their hearts, made several reckless personal finance and business decisions and now we have to bear the brunt of their burden. Then add that to taking care of siblings, in-laws and outlaws."

"And Lord knows, there are many outlaws hanging out in Sherwood Forest, pulling some major Robin Hood stunts," Hassan concurred as both men laughed.

"But guy, that thing you said made a lot of sense. When you have dependents, you can depend on them to leave dents in your finances. Your dependents will leave dents in your finances. Chai! No worries, that's why God made us men, He knows we can handle it. Thanks for hearing me out. Make I go finish work," Hassan said as he stood to leave.

As he watched his friend walk away, Ezzy couldn't help thinking about what Hassan had said.

Poverty stress. That's what it is. *I wonder what Toks would think about this.*

GULF CAPITAL.
SOMA'S OFFICE.
2.17pm

Soma could smell Amaka a mile away and so could everyone else. Her cologne was so distinct, that everyone in the Branch caught a whiff of her before she ever showed up.

"Somalicious," cooed Amaka as she leaned in to peck Soma on both cheeks. "I've got gist for you and it's fresh off the press."

"I'd be surprised if you didn't," Soma replied, cheekily.

"Besides, it's lunch time, and you're buying," Amaka smiled as she reached for her Alexander McQueen bag and began strutting to the exit.

CAFÉ NEO

"These frappucinos are to die for!" Amaka gushed as she sipped her latte.

"Yep! Oya Amaka, spill it. What's the latest scoop? And whose dirt have you dug up?" Soma couldn't bear the suspense anymore.

"I knew you couldn't resist," Amaka smiled as she pulled her chair closer.

"Hmm. Soma, you wouldn't believe what these ears of mine have been listening to since I was transferred to the Treasury department."

"I'm all ears," Soma replied.

"I overheard Madam P and Aunty Booki talking about their last trip to the UK and how they splurged at Selfridges and cleaned out Prada."

"Those two dey overdo sef. Na only dem waka come?" Soma scoffed.

It was a well-known fact that Madam P and Aunty Booki had friends in high places and were deemed untouchable due to their close ties to several political heavyweights who constantly ensured their accounts were bursting at the seams with transactions; and since the bank gave commissions to staff that brought in high volume transactions, Madam P and Aunty Booki were always, literally, smiling to the bank, much to the chagrin of their co-workers.

"You should check out all the stuff they posted on Instagram. The things they bought could open several chains of stores," Amaka said.

"Show offs!" Soma snorted disdainfully.

"Oh well, we can't knock their hustle. They've earned it. Sha, here's praying that we'll someday hit the big leagues and be flossing Elie Tahari dresses and Manolo Blahnik's," Amaka toasted with her glass raised.

"I'll drink to that." They clicked their glasses.

"But there's more," Amaka whispered conspiratorially, "you won't believe what's going on with kids of today."

"What's going on?" Soma asked.

Amaka signaled the waiter for a refill of her frappucino.

"There I was minding my business when I overheard Madam P telling Aunty Booki about how she'd taken her kids on a trip to Disneyland in Florida, and when they'd returned, she had a few friends over who brought their own kids on a play date and overheard the children talking."

"That's not a big deal, Amaka. Kids do that all the time," Soma countered.

"I haven't finished jor."

Amaka dusted her dress as the waiter returned with her order."Oya sorry, continue."

"As I was saying, she overhears her children talking about their Disneyland trip and then, one of the other kids asks them what section of the plane they sat in."

"No way!"

"Way! And when they said they flew Economy, the other kids started laughing because their parents made sure they only fly Business or First Class."

"See pikin wey dey craze o!"

"That's not all," Amaka continued. "As you can imagine, na so Madam P pikin come ask im mama why dem no dey fly Business class go Yankee in front of Madam P friends."

"I no go woz am better slap?" Soma replied, shaking vigorously.

"Babe, na so Madam P tell im pikin say e no matter where you sit for plane, as long as say all of us go land the same time."

"The pikin gree?" Soma asked.

"Gree wetin? Na so the boy come dey cry!"

"Oh, Amaka. I don tell you say I go woz am better slap!" Soma gestured animatedly, simulating a slap on the face.

"But seriously," Amaka continued. "The peer pressure is unbelievable. So it's no longer good enough that we can travel to other parts of the world and purchase a seat on a plane, we're now judged by our seating location."

"It's a crazy world we live in," Soma concurred as she sipped her frappucino.

"I'm telling you. I mean my sister has a lot of stress because her children's school often schedules excursions to foreign countries and she has a hard time keeping up."

"Keeping up with the Joneses abi Kardashians, you mean?" Soma scoffed.

"Abeg, Amaka, if she no get the money, make she commot them from the school. Abi na by force to go Yankee for excursion, when La Campagne Tropicana never finish?"

"I don tell her tire, my mouth don dey pain me," Amaka sighed.

"Make she dey there," Soma retorted. "Honestly, I sometimes think that the education we claim to be giving our kids is less for their academic aptitude and more of a social status thing so we can claim bragging rights that our kids go abroad on excursions and the likes. Schools today are status products with educational benefits."

"Preach!" Amaka waved her hand in the air.

"My dear, when you start praying for what you ordinarily should be able to pay for, then it's time to make a change."

"Preach on, Preacher!" Amaka waved again.

"Don't buy anything that needs prayer to pay for," Soma continued. "Can I get a witness from somebody?"

"Hallelujah!" Amaka chorused as both ladies laughed.

"Babe, make we dey go before they kick us out for disturbing the peace" Soma giggled.

She signaled the waiter. "Can we have our bill please?"

CASA DE TOKS

Ezzy had just finished recounting what had transpired earlier with Hassan when Soma walked in.

"Hey babe." Ezzy kissed his wife on the cheek.

The process of getting them to become financially fit had made them even closer and more connected with each other.

"Hi Soma," Toks smiled as he poured her a glass of wine.

"What have I missed?" Soma asked. Ezzy quickly brought her up to speed.

"Hmm," she murmured. "Sounds pretty much like my day--" as she filled them in on her conversation with Amaka.

"What do you think, Coach?" Ezzy asked.

Toks took a sip from his glass, reached for his peanuts and began to speak.

"For starters, Ezzy, I totally agree. That's definitely poverty stress."

Ezzy jumped up and began to dance around the room. "Finally, I've taught Toks something," he laughed.

"Too bad this conversation isn't being recorded, now you have no proof that it ever happened," Toks joked.

"Damn! Na true sha." Ezzy's jig came to an abrupt end.

"Don't worry, love," Soma grinned, "I'm a witness. So if Toks ever writes a book on Financial Fitness and uses your principle, he'll have to compensate you."

"That'd be the day." Toks swirled his drink with a mischievous grin plastered on his face. "If you two lovebirds are quite finished, I'd like to get back to analyzing those scenarios you brought up."

"Go right ahead, Toks," Soma smiled, pulling her husband to the sofa.

"Where were we?"

"I'd given you a million dollar concept called poverty stress," Ezzy said, wincing immediately as Soma punched him playfully on the shoulder.

"Joker!" Toks grinned, then continued. "Ezzy is – and I can't believe I'm saying this – absolutely right about poverty stress--"

Ezzy was about to leap from the sofa again and run a victory lap around the living room when Soma pulled him by the ear.

Toks continued, giggling at the couple's antics. "Have you ever noticed crabs in a barrel before?"

Ezzy scratched his head and stared at Toks blankly.

Soma spoke, "Yes, Toks, I have. What about them?"

"Fantastic, Soma. Have you noticed that when harvesting crab, the crab as a group will pull down any crab that starts to climb out of the barrel in an attempt to be the first out of the barrel that holds them in, hence the phrase crabs-in-a-barrel?"

"Hmm. That's true," Soma concurred.

"Crabs in a barrel perfectly epitomizes the concept of poverty stress.

"So just as one individual seems to be getting out of the barrel of poverty, there are at least ten other folks whose poverty weight causes them to fall back to the depths of poverty; so at the end, no one is truly free."

"Oh wow. Poverty weight. That's deep," Ezzy said as he scratched his head.

"It gets deeper," Toks continued. "What the crabs fail to realize is that two poor people can never help each other; they forget that pulling somebody down will never help you reach the top."

"Word!" Soma couldn't help but thump the table.

"Toks, you've got to repeat that last statement about poor people," she said.

"Two poor people cannot help each other," he reiterated. *"You can't help the poor if you're one of them"*

Ezzy couldn't resist jumping in. "Man, Toks…that thing you said about poverty weight struck me."

"The floor's yours, Ezzy," Toks said.

"You said that as one individual seems to be getting out of the barrel of poverty, there are at least ten other folks whose poverty weight causes them to fall back to the depths of poverty; so at the end, no one is truly free."

"I did indeed," Toks concurred as he took a sip of his wine.

"You know, I work out as often as I can--"

"Could've fooled me," Toks grinned, "that stomach looks more like a beer barrel than a six pack."

"You've got jokes," Ezzy smiled, rubbing his slightly round paunch. He winked, "It's a sign of wealth."

"How ironic," Toks replied sarcastically.

"Nice one!" Ezzy high-fived Toks for the witty retort.

"But go on, man, seems you're on to something," Toks said.

"As I was saying, I was thinking of the analogy of bench pressing. If I'm on my A game, I can bench press ninety kilograms; it'll stress me out, but I can work it, although with a lot of groaning and sweating. Anything less than eighty kilograms is usually a walk in the park, but anything above and beyond my capacity will probably knock me out. So I figure that too many of us are trying to carry poverty weight that's beyond our capacity; but because, like the average weight lifter, we don't want to cop out or admit that it's beyond us or maybe it's our ego, we attempt to lift it and get embarrassed as we choke under the pressure."

"Aww, now I know why you've stopped going to the gym," Soma laughed.

Ezzy blushed.

"But seriously Ezzy, that's definitely a great way to look at it," Toks agreed.

"The greater the poverty weight you carry, the quicker you end up poor," concurred Soma.

"The best way to help another person out of poverty is to get out first and send down a ladder when you're out," Ezzy continued.

"I couldn't agree more," Toks replied.

Soma had a few reservations.

"But guys, I think we're forgetting something important. How do we communicate all this to our extended families? This is Africa, worse still, this is Nigeria. We're built on a long standing system or institution of dependency. Most of our parents sent us to school, not necessarily to get an education or to invest into our future; we were their investment to the future they wanted, and with every investment, there must be dividends. And now, as far as they're concerned, it's payback time. So bringing it right where we are; you know how momsie always calls several times a month, with one problem or the other; and there's your brother, Raymond, who still hasn't gotten a job, but comes over every week to get an allowance and how we have to lend a helping hand every other day. Argh! It just goes on and on. How do we handle that, knowing that all these needs are valid?"

Toks walked to the patio and gestured for Ezzy and Soma to join him. Staring at his beachfront property, he focused his attention on the cityscape beyond him.

"Tell me, guys. What do you see?" he asked.

"A massive beachfront property that my landlord's house could comfortably fit into six times over," Ezzy chuckled.

"More like seven," Toks joked. "I've seen where you live."

"Touché!" Ezzy grinned.

Toks turned his attention to Soma who appeared lost in thought.

"Soma, what about you? What do you see?"

Soma inhaled deeply.

"I see two parallels. On one side, epitomized by your beach house, I see peace and tranquility. On the other side, epitomized by the city and the traffic building up, I see chaos and stress. On this side, I see the lifestyle of the rich and on the other side, the hustle and grind of the poor. Here, I see money working for you, there I see people running around to work for money.

"I used to have a lot of bias towards rich people, now I know that I had a negative money mentality towards anyone that was rich. In fact, my money mentality was *I'm sure he stole it* or *she was probably lucky or born into a wealthy family* or *she's probably sleeping with some rich man that's dashing her money.*

"Their wealth reminded me of my insecurity, so I would hustle and grind to measure up by getting the nice jewelry, shoes and bags. I looked like a million bucks, but inside, I was still incredibly poor. My lack of esteem was over compensated with lavish shopping sprees, purchasing things on credit that I couldn't afford. I mean, just recently, a blogger purchased a home in one of these plush estates, and man, the vitriol and beef she got was so palpable. You thought they'd be happy for her because she'd made her way out of the barrel, but these people, abi, crabs went on a hate fest, trying to pull her back to the bottom, accusing her of sleeping her way to the top and many other fabricated stories, excusing away her success, only because she had made it to the top. So now, my money mentality has changed; I recognize that a rich person is a poor person that got tired of being broke, stopped explaining away his poverty and learned the secrets of being rich. Using Toks' crabs in a barrel analogy, a rich person is a crab that got tired of being at the bottom of the barrel, struggling for scarce resources with other crabs, decided to climb out, and eventually made his way out of the barrel, irrespective of the claws of the other crabs trying to pull him down."

"Wow!" Ezzy exclaimed, in shock, looking at Soma with new found respect. Staring at Soma, he suddenly realized he had put her in a box and labelled it 'wife' and 'mother' and had forgotten there were many other important labels, aspects and appellations to her that he had taken for granted.

"Somaliscious! Somali sumptuous! That's some amazing insight." He punctuated his praise with kisses on his wife's cheek.

"I agree!" Toks grinned, grateful for the life he had been given to impact the lives of so many. "Soma, that was so profound. I couldn't have said it better myself."

"Thank you, Toks," Soma said, blushing. "You guys are making me feel like a superstar. What do you expect when I roll with you heavy hitters? I have no choice but to throw down."

"Girl, you definitely threw down right there." Ezzy smiled as he hugged his wife.

"So Toks, back to my question, how do we deal with this culture of dependency?"

Toks reached for his glass. "Just say no."

"No? Haaaaa Toks, maybe you didn't quite get the question."

"I got it crystal clear, dear." Toks smiled.

"But seriously, Toks. You can't expect me to tell my momsie that I don't have o. She won't stand for it."

"Then you'll have to take the fall for it and drag around your poverty weight without complaining. Listen guys, I know exactly what you're talking about, you can't begin to imagine what I have to deal with every month, and I'm not even speaking about staff salaries."

"So how do you deal with it?" Ezzy inquired.

"Simple," Toks replied. "You remember your SIT plan?"

"How could we forget?" Ezzy answered. "That was our single biggest stop-gap mechanism from going under."

"Good to hear it," Toks replied. "Now, remember I said that if you don't make plans for money, money will definitely make its plans for you? So what you need to do first, is after sorting out *Do Not Touch* investments, and it's time to deal with recurrent expenses such as housekeeping, fuel, etc., create a mini section for dependents and here's the kicker, apportion a certain fixed amount to it."

"But Toks," Soma interjected. "We already do that. What I'm asking is how do we reduce the poverty weight we carry?"

"Again, I say, just say no. And before you disagree, Soma, hear me out."

Soma smiled and reclined into her seat.

"No. It's such a simple word, but it carries so much essence and power. It simply means the right to refuse. Why are we so uncomfortable with saying no? It's simple. We're concerned about how the other party will perceive us – probably as inadequate or incapable – and that's not good for our carefully manicured and cultivated reputation. We don't say no, because of how we feel. We don't say no, because there's a small place in our ego or pride that wants to say, *I got this, I can handle this, I've got it covered.* We don't say no because we don't want the other party to think less of us or look down on us. When we don't say no, it's less about the person you're refusing, and more about you."

"Hmm. True though," Ezzy murmured as Soma sat lost in thought.

"But I'm gonna say something that might go down the wrong way, but I'll say it anyway. If you were to, God forbid, lose your job today, how many of those dependents of yours will pester you for money?"

"Not one of them!" Soma exclaimed.

"Why not?" Toks asked.

"Them no get brain? It's pretty obvious that the brook has run dry," Soma said.

"So what do they do when their brook has run dry?" Toks asked.

"Find another brook," Ezzy chimed in.

"Exactly. So what I'm suggesting is that if you can't outright refuse, in order to alleviate the pressure on your finances, it's okay to simulate a spell or two of a dry season, where for reasons best known to you, you simply say no."

"That's sneaky," Ezzy grinned. "And I love it. Now we know what to say when your momsie calls or when Raymond shows up."

"Think about it, guys," Toks continued. "I do agree, as Soma said, that those needs are valid. But here's the thing, they're not urgent to you. You have to recognize there's only one Savior and you're not Him. Now, I'm not suggesting that you be insensitive to their struggles or challenges, but you've got your own struggles too. And here's the kicker, if you got into trouble, how many of your dependents would be able to help you?"

"Absolutely none!" Soma said.

"Oyo lo wa," Ezzy scoffed. "You're on your own."

"Exactly!" Toks concurred. "They'd mourn with you, or to be more exact, they'd mourn the loss of your income and benefits to them and after a while, move on to a more profitable brook that's still got some juice flowing through it."

"Besides," Ezzy interjected, “heaven helps those who help themselves."

"Indeed," Toks concurred. "One of the major reasons a lot of aspiring middle class families struggle is simply because they spend tomorrow's money today taking care of issues of yesterday."

"Whoop!" Soma shrieked. "That's a tweetable right there." She brought out her phone and typed:

We spend tomorrow's money today taking care of issues of yesterday.

"Absolutely," Toks said as he signaled for the butler to refill the drinks. "Or put it another way, if you eat your future in your present, you will go back to your past hungry."

"For the love of God and His holy angels!" Ezzy exclaimed. "Toks, how do you come up with this stuff?"

"I could tell you a bunch of different answers: research, life experience and all, but I'm gonna chalk it up to *God speaks and I echo*."

"I agree," Ezzy said. "It had to be the Big Man upstairs. I know you're definitely not that smart."

"And neither are you." Toks smiled.

Soma interrupted their reverie. "Excuse me, Toks, but what you said was just so profound. I can't seem to get it out of my mind. We spend tomorrow's money today taking care of issues of yesterday. That's so true for me... for us. A lot of our debt and liability is simply because of poor financial management decisions we made in the past."

"Now imagine what could happen when you make the right decisions?" Toks said. "Life would be a heck of a lot easier and a lot less dramatic. But now, there's a flip side to what I said previously, which is that money made yesterday and invested today will give you a better life tomorrow."

"Another tweetable," Soma cheered as she captured Toks' thoughts. They were way too invaluable to forget.

It's no small wonder he's as successful as he is, Soma thought. *You can bump into money on the road to success, but wealth must be searched out.*

"Damn!" Ezzy whistled. "Toks, that was deep. You're definitely in the zone, downloading some inspiration from The Big Man Upstairs. *Money made yesterday and invested today will give you a better life tomorrow.*"

"Yeah, I know," Toks replied, "there's been a lot to think about. Remember that you're one bad decision away from becoming a dependent yourself."

"Tweetable" Soma said, grinning

"You're one bad decision away from becoming a dependent yourself."

"Damn right" Ezzy agreed.

Toks got off the sofa and stretched.

"So, what's the most important thing you've learned today? I'll begin".

"*A rich man is a poor man that got tired of being broke.*"

"Whoop! Whoop!" Soma exclaimed. "I've been quoted!" She laughed as she did a little jig around the men.

"Ezzy? What about you?" Toks asked.

"*We spend tomorrow's money today taking care of issues of yesterday.* That really resonated with me. It's given me a lot of food for thought."

"Soma? What's your tweetable moment?"

"*Just say NO and more importantly, you're one bad decision away from becoming a dependent yourself*."

"And may we never depend on those who once depended on us," Ezzy said.

"I'll drink to that" Toks said, raising his glass.

"Amen!" They clinked their glasses together.

TOTAL MONEY WORKOUT

1. List your dependents whose poverty weight is stopping you from growing financially.
2. Why can't you say NO to them? Be honest. It's time to confront yourself.
3. If you got into financial trouble, how many of your present dependents could possibly help you?
4. What are you going to different now?

CHAPTER EIGHT

WHEN MONEY DOESN'T PAY ATTENTION

Secret 8: "Create the value that commands the attention of money"

"Ol' boy o! See as dollar dey take our money play ball," Hassan remarked as he flipped through the financial section of the newspaper.

"Guy, na so I see am," Ezzy replied.

The economy seemed to be in dire straits. Due to falling oil prices and a massive drain on the nation's economy by many corrupt government officials and decades of bad economic policies, the Nigerian currency, the Naira had taken a beating and lost more than a third of its value in the international market.

"Na to dey earn in Dollars be dat," Hassan said as he closed the paper.

"Dude, that's the only way to go," Ezzy replied. "We need to figure out a way to capitalize on this crisis."

Both men sighed, knowing they had no clue how to do that.

SOMA's OFFICE

"No! It can't be true! You can't be serious."

Everyone turned to look at Soma who was screaming frantically into the phone.

"Where are you? Stay there. I'm coming"

And with that, Soma hurriedly walked out of the building and got into her car.

"Oh God," she prayed. "Please don't let it be true. Let this be one big joke. But if it is, I'm going to wring her perfumed neck."

FOUR POINTS BY SHERATON LAGOS
43 minutes later

"Babe, are you okay?" Soma asked. "I'm sorry I'm late. I drove as fast as I could."

Amaka barely noticed Soma. She looked blank, gazing into the distance, her hands firmly fixed on an empty wine glass with a half empty bottle of wine in front of her.

"Amaka!" Soma shook her friend out of her reverie.

"Hey you..." Amaka slurred. "Didn't know you were here."

"Amaka, what's wrong? It's barely noon and you're drunk? What's going on?"

"Abegggiiii. Spare me the lecture. You'd be drunk too if you'd lost your job."

Soma took the wine glass from Amaka and embraced her as she began to cry.

Soma signaled for the waiter. "Can I have a cup of your strongest coffee? Black, no sugar or cream."

Turning back to her friend. "Amaka, talk to me. What happened? How could you have lost your job?"

"Soma, I'm finished. Soma, where am I going to start from? I'm 37 years old with 2 kids, a husband that barely has his act together and a mortgage. I've been on this job for 10 years and I'm only one level higher than you and you've been here for only seven abi eight? This job is all I've known and what pays the bills. I have more loans than I can possibly pay off. I'm still paying off my car loan and the stupid holiday we took to Greece; all this time my husband has just been forming 'CEO' and not even doing business. I've been bailing him out every month for the last one and a half years to pay his staff salaries and office rent and I took a loan to fund it. He keeps talking about the contracts he's pursuing and how they'll soon click and we'll be on Easy Street, but it's been almost 2 years and not one deal has pulled through, and the joker decided against my better judgment to get an office on the Island, so he could brag to his useless friends that he's arrived. I just paid Chisom's first term fees into that posh secondary school I told you about, how will I sort out her second term fees? Now I've lost my livelihood. Soma, am I not finished?"

From Soma's point of view, Amaka was clearly *finished*. But telling her that wasn't going to offer any comfort to Amaka and she knew it.

"Chai. Pele. Pele." Soma continued muttering as the waiter arrived with her order. She quickly poured Amaka a cup of coffee while gathering her thoughts.

"Amaka, walk me through what happened."

Fighting back her tears, Amaka began to speak:

"Soma, if anyone had told me that I'd lose my job this morning, I would've called them a liar. Nothing, I mean nothing, could have prepared me for the shock I received when I headed out to work this morning. I mean, I didn't even get the courtesy shock of you know, the usual, not being able to log in to my computer. I got an SMS. Soma, an SMS! I mean, who does that?" Amaka hissed.

"Aaaah? SMS? Wait, Amaka, so you got an SMS saying you'd been laid off?"

Soma asked.

"Abeg. Say it well jor. I was sacked jare, which one be laid off? You don't know that when you're laid off, you get benefits for leaving the system but when you're sacked, you're owing the system and you'll be lucky to leave with the clothes on your back."

"Sorry, love," apologized Soma.

"I'm sorry I'm being bitchy," Amaka replied. "But I've never been sacked before and at this stage of my life. I'm struggling to figure out what my next move is."

"I understand." Soma hugged her friend. "You mentioned that you got an SMS saying you were laid off, sorry, I mean, sacked..."

"No. The SMS didn't say I was sacked. It only said I should come to the Head Office for a 10:45am meeting."

"Oh okay."

"So I drove to Head Office and took the elevator to Manpower Development and all this time, I'm thinking maybe it's about Ronke's performance appraisal, since I'm her supervisor."

"Yeah, I remember that case," Soma replied. "She accused you being vindictive or something like that?"

"See me, see trouble, my sister. Don't mind her. I'll still show her in this bank," Amaka said and took a sharp breath as the words sank in.

"Chai, Soma. I'm finished," Amaka said for the second time. "I'm so finished that I can't even start with this babe."

"Let's not focus on that," Soma said, quickly steering the conversation back to the main issue.

"Shit. My makeup is running from all this crying," Amaka said, cleaning her mascara.

"So what happened when you got to Manpower Development?"

"I thought I was going to meet with Bello, Segun or maybe Nkeiru, but once I got there, one lady – I think she's new, I didn't recognize her – asked for my name, handed me an envelope and walked away."

"Didn't she say anything?" Soma asked.

"Not one word," sniffed Amaka as she dabbed her eyes and blew her nose.

In all the years she had known her, Soma had never seen Amaka in such bad shape.

How could this have happened to Amaka? she thought. *This wasn't fair. Amaka was good at her job, I mean, sure she wasn't a super performer, but who was? She got by as best she could, and despite her penchant for all things bright and beautiful, Amaka definitely wasn't a slouch; but to get fired in these uncertain economic times? She hadn't previously known the state of Amaka's finances, but hearing her talk about it made Soma's heart ache for her best friend. How would she cope?*

Sadly, Soma realized that if it hadn't been for Toks' Total Money Workout sessions, she would've been in really bad shape.

"Jesus, thank you," she muttered under her breath as she squeezed her friend's hand.

"Soma, I'm finished o. How do I dig myself out of this grave?" Amaka wailed as the tears started to slide down her mascara stained cheeks.

Soma held Amaka close and as she felt the tremors, Soma too began to cry.

CASA DE EZZY
7:23pm

"Hey Toks, what a pleasant surprise! What brings you to our neck of the woods?" Ezzy grinned as he ushered Toks in to his living room.

"I wanted to see how the other half lived," Toks said as he slapped Ezzy on the back.

"Nice! 1 - 0. See this guy, you don dey yab me, abi?"

"I come in peace. See, I come bearing gifts," Toks grinned as he handed Ezzy a bottle of wine.

"Fantastic, we can cease all hostilities until after we have drunk to peace," Ezzy said as he reached for the ice pack.

"Where's Soma?"

"She should be home any moment now.

“How's Barbara and the kids? I haven't seen them in a long while, at least not since we started our coaching sessions," Ezzy asked, referring to Toks' family.

"They're fantastic!" Toks replied as he sipped his drink. "The kids are in boarding school."

"Bad guy, I'm sure they're in one posh secondary school where they have nannies and people doing their laundry. Chai, when I grow up sha, I'll be a big boy too."

"Sorry to burst your bubble, bro. They're not in any such school. Barbs and I realized that while money can be passed on to your kids, financial intelligence isn't exactly inherited. It must be deliberately instituted."

"Hmmm. That's deep. Oro jade, ase tele. Abeg, wait a second, let me record our conversation. Soma will murder me if she doesn't get the full gist of our convo" Ezzy said as he fiddled with his phone.

"Okay, I'm good. You can say that last part again."

"Money can be passed on to your kids, but financial intelligence isn't inherited. It must be deliberately instituted."

"That's true," Ezzy concurred. "If Soma were here, she'd say that's a tweetable right there. *Financial intelligence isn't inherited, it must be deliberately instituted.*"

Toks continued.

"Now, even though the kids have had some measure of...comfort, from an early age, we focused on raising them with strict moral values."

"That's important," Ezzy agreed. "I've seen so many spoiled rich kids who just live off Daddy's money, with a sense of entitlement and have no skills whatsoever."

"Yeah. So Barbs and I wanted to continue that legacy. So we sent them to my secondary school. They're big on education and very deliberate in installing a moral code in the kids."

"But couldn't you have found a school on the Island that ticks all those boxes for you?" Ezzy asked.

"Perhaps, but here's my challenge with those schools. Sure, the education is top notch, no doubt about that. My issue is they usually cater to a certain class of children from privileged or similar backgrounds. It perpetuates a class system. Now, there's nothing wrong with that, if that's what floats your boat. But I feel it sequesters the kids from experiencing life as it really is without all the frills, makeup, foundation and eye liner; meeting kids from all sorts of life experiences gives them an appreciation for what they have, and also teaches them life skills from an early age. Hard work doesn't kill. Let the children learn to hustle before they go to any university of their choice. My kids shouldn't be asking me to send them money every time they have a need, they must be able to create the value that commands the attention of money."

"Jesus Christ! Toks, that was deep! Create the value that commands the attention of money! Wow!" Ezzy exclaimed. "And all this time, I'd been aspiring to send my kids to such schools and now, you've given me another paradigm--"

"Babe, if you see the car that's parked downstairs ehn, it looks like one of those cars in those *Fast and Furious* movies." Soma said; excitedly gesticulating as she walked into the living room.

"I hope it's not being a nuisance," Toks grinned.

"Oops. Hi Toks." Soma said, visibly embarrassed "What a pleasant surprise."

"Yeah, that's what he said," Toks replied, pointing to Ezzy.

"You guys are enjoying, looks like I've missed a lot of gist. Let me take a look at the kids and pull off these heels, I'll be right back."

"Take your time," Toks replied as Ezzy kissed his wife.

When she was out of earshot, Toks winked at his friend. "I see the romance has returned to the castle."

"Man, whoever said money was the root of all evil, was spot on," Ezzy grinned as he took another sip of wine.

"Technically, it's the lack of money that's the root of evil, but hey, point taken," Toks smiled.

"Dude, do you know that most of our spats and fights were money related? Now, we've got greater peace. It's not like we're earning more, but since we started this journey with you and have started getting our shit together, we actually have less cause for drama; and when the urges rear their ugly heads to entice us to splurge, we actually team up like Voltron and just help each other out. It's done a lot for our marriage and the sex, you don't wanna know..."

"You're right, I don't wanna know," Toks said as they both laughed.

"Don't wanna know what?" Soma asked as she sat, snuggling close to her husband.

"Err...Nothing important. How was your day?" Ezzy asked as he ruffled her hair.

"Worst day ever!" Soma exclaimed. She began to recount the experiences of the day as Toks and Ezzy listened, transfixed.

"Wow." Toks exhaled as Soma finished her tale.

"...That sucks," Ezzy concurred, finishing Toks' statement.

"Here's the key question I'd like you to answer, Soma. What transferable skills does she have?"

"I'm not sure I understand your question, Toks," she replied.

"Okay, let me put this into perspective while I stretch my legs," Toks said as he rose from the sofa. He walked around the living room, taking long strides as he paced the floor.

"Here's my frustration with most employees and for some reason, I can't seem to get over it. Most employees don't recognize the gift they've been given! It's a matter of perspective. Most employees are very myopic and can't see past the nose on their face. They don't train themselves unless their organization sends them on training! I mean, come on guys, no disrespect to you; but you both work for organizations; when was the last time you paid to attend a training that would improve your performance on the job?"

"Err...let me see...never," Ezzy said cheekily.

"I paid to attend *House of Tara's* makeup class last year," Soma said, raising her hand.

"Nice try, Soma, but are you in the beauty business?" Toks asked.

"No, but I'm interested in makeup--" Soma replied.

"And that, ladies and gents, is the million dollar answer!" Toks said, clapping his hands excitedly.

"Makeup is the answer? Am I missing something?" Ezzy asked, scratching his head.

"Apart from your mind? Nah, you're just fine," Toks smiled as he high-fived Ezzy.

"Chai! 2 - 0. Well played." Ezzy clapped.

"You two are at it again," Soma smiled. "Don't you ever stop?"

"Only after Toks starts," Ezzy grinned.

"That's because you can't finish!" Toks yelled, doing a victory lap around the apartment.

"Chai! 3 - 0." Ezzy moaned, pouring himself and Soma a drink.

"Oya Toks, could you please finish what you started? What's the million dollar answer?"

"It's *interest* and *self-interest,*" he responded.

"Err," Ezzy interrupted, "ain't they one and the same?"

"Not quite. Let me explain. Let's use Soma's answer as the analogy. The reason she took Tara's make up classes is because it does two things. She's *interested* in makeup and beauty and it also meets her *self-interest,* whether it is to be able to apply her makeup better in order to stand out or perhaps to understand the business of makeup and beauty. Am I right, Soma?"

"Sadly," Soma smiled ruefully.

"Hmm...I see where you're going with this," Ezzy said.

"So to get Soma's undivided attention, it must involve Soma's *fascination,* which is her interest and her *motivation,* which is her self-interest. So put it this way, focus is when fascination meets with motivation," Toks said.

"Tweetable! *Focus is when fascination meets with motivation."*

"So what you're saying is as long as the corporate interest doesn't match Soma's self-interest, she'll not be interested," Ezzy chimed in.

"Absolutely! People only invest in their self-interest. So as long as Soma can achieve her self-interest without being invested in the company's interest, then she's just coasting. So if another vehicle that helps her meet her self-interest come along, as long as she's not fascinated with her company, she's going to jump ship."

"But Toks, how is that a bad thing?" asked Soma. "Shouldn't I look out for Number One?"

"There's nothing wrong with looking out for Number One as you put it, but what about the disservice to your organization? Here's my grouse with employees, and don't forget I've been one, so I'm not sitting on some moral high horse. Let me put it this way, how much did your company earn during its last financial year?"

Ezzy and Soma exchanged furtive glances.

"What's going on? Cat got your tongue?" Toks asked. "Okay, next question. What's your company's monthly fuel bill?"

Soma raised her hand and on second thought, put her hand down.

"Final question. What's your company's monthly internet bill?"

Ezzy scratched his head nervously.

"So why don't you have the answers to my three questions? What's the common denominator?"

"No interest," Soma muttered under her breath.

"Sorry dear, I missed that. Could you speak a little louder?" Toks asked

"There's no interest in what the company does," Soma reiterated.

"Interest creates ownership. And don't forget that many times, this information is in your company's annual reports. But if it were your business. If you owned the company, would you know what your internet or fuel bills cost?"

"Definitely," Ezzy said, sufficiently chastened. "But bro, it's not as easy as you make it out to seem. Sometimes, we've got bad bosses who work us to the bone, some guys are literally slave drivers. They feel because they're paying you a salary, they own you."

"I don't agree with that philosophy, but here's what I think. The reward of being an employee is not how much you make, but who you become through the process."

"Oooh! I knew I was forgetting something," Soma said as she leapt off the sofa. "Toks, hold that thought, let me get my coaching book."

Ezzy looked out of the window and wondered how many opportunities to learn the business of advertising he had thrown away by constantly focusing on his paycheck.

"I'm back," Soma said, bounding into the room. "Toks, can you repeat the last sentence?"

"Sure. *The reward of being an employee is not how much you make, but who you become through the process.*"

"That's deep," Soma said as she scribbled the words in her notepad.

"So here's my big idea, guys. As long as the goose lays the golden eggs, no one cares how the goose is fed. How does an employee who has absolutely no interest or understanding in how a company he's spent two to five years working in operates, expect to magically build a successful enterprise? That's pretty selfish and I dare say, far out. I mean no disrespect guys, but I'm sure you've got an entrepreneurial itch that you want to scratch someday. But you don't realize your company's paying you to learn its business and trade secrets. Your organization has given you an exclusive back stage pass to go behind the scenes and understand their entire value chain. But most employees don't realize that.

They only learn the ropes for their job description, and unfortunately, most of those skills aren't transferable; and sadly, because most employees don't have a sense of vision, they give the least level of performance to their jobs. They do enough to keep their jobs, but unfortunately, not enough to get promoted, so they wallow in self-pity, not realizing the power they've been looking for was in their hands all the time. Then one day, like your friend, life happens and then they realize they have no skills, just a life experience of doing the same thing for several years."

"Chaiiiiiii! I just had an epiphany." Soma screamed. "In my branch, there's an ATM custodian who's been on the same level for ten years. She's constantly complaining about being shafted by the company for not promoting her, especially when she has to come to work during weekends when the ATM runs out of cash."

"She's lucky she has a job," Toks growled. "No disrespect to her, but it's not rocket science managing an ATM. I mean, how hard could it be? Besides, that particular skill might be outsourced to machines in three to five years. But let's say it takes a year to learn this particular ATM custodian thingy, tell me how this skill is transferable to a different organization? Soma, I hate to break it to you, but this lady you mentioned doesn't have ten years' experience; she has one year experience of doing the same thing for 10 years."

"Shiiiiiiiitttttt," exclaimed Ezzy. "Toks, that's just cold."

"Perhaps, but it's true. You can't expect to be a successful entrepreneur if you've been a crappy employee. If you haven't been faithful with your nine to five, how on earth will you manage a twenty-four/seven? Besides, you know what they say about karma..."

"What goes around comes around?" Ezzy asked.

"No. She's a bitch," Soma concluded.

TOTAL MONEY WORKOUT

1. Are you deliberately doing anything to pass financial intelligence down to your kids or dependents?
1. What specific things could you do to pass down financial intelligence to your dependents, and particularly kids around you?
2. On a scale of 1 to 100, rate your present level of commitment to your job.
3. What can you do different to improve your level of commitment?

CHAPTER NINE

MY MONEY AND YOUR MONEY NO BE MATE

Secret 9: "If your take home pay can't take you home, then change your address."

"Young man. What are you doing up?" Soma asked as she stirred to see Ezzy sitting on the edge of the bed.

"Don't worry, babe, go back to sleep, it's nothing."

"Nothing, and you're up at…" Soma reached for her phone. "…2.17am? Babe, what's wrong?"

"Nothing to worry your pretty little head about. Go back to sleep."

"I can't sleep, besides, neither can you. So you might as well tell me what's bugging you."

Ezzy began pacing the floor. "I've just been thinking of all the stuff that Toks said."

"Yeah, it's a lot to digest," Soma agreed

"I just feel like I've passed over so many opportunities."

Soma sighed "Well, we're all wiser in hindsight. What matters now are the steps we take going forward that will determine where we end up."

"I know. But is it enough? I mean, babe, look at me. I'm almost halfway past 40. How much time could I possibly have left in me to pursue this Advertising job of mine? I'm just a glorified sales man and pencil pusher."

"Don't say that," Soma said.

"It's the ugly truth, like that your Life Strategist would say. I've been following him on Instagram and checking out his podcasts. He makes some sense though. But the fact is, I feel like I've wasted the time I've had and I feel like I don't have much left."

"God forbid. You have time in Jesus name."

"Oooohhhh, leave that side. But sha, Amen, before I enter one chance. But you catch my drift?"

"Mgbe onye ji tete bu ututu ya."

"Err...Google Translate please?"

"When you wake up is when your morning begins."

"Well, that may be so, but I feel like I've overslept."

"So what do you want to do? You just can't quit your job, you have responsibilities."

"So what do I do? Should I remain in a job, playing a position that I'm not suited for, being criticized for not doing well, trying to run down the clock, hoping my manager doesn't substitute me or decides never to play me again or puts me on a free transfer?"

"Err...Google Translate please. I don't speak Premiership."

"I'm in the wrong position in the wrong place and not getting the right results."

"Should we talk to Toks about this? Maybe it's the onset of midlife crisis."

"Babe, Toks and I are the same age, so I know it's not midlife crisis."

"You just feel you're not at the same stage," Soma said.

"We're not at the same stage and neither is our money. My money is like a roadside beggar compared to his."

"So you feel like your money and his money no be mate," Soma said

"I couldn't have said it any better myself."

"Don't worry. Let's go to bed, it'll all be clearer in the morning" Soma said, pulling her husband back to bed.

"I sure as hell hope so" Ezzy said, pulling up the covers.

THE LOUNGE

"I thought I'd find you here," Toks said, pulling up a chair. He looked around, noting the half empty bottle of whiskey. "Looks like you've been here for a while."

"How did you find- never mind, Soma told you."

"Yeah, she said you were worried about something, she mentioned a midlife crisis. Aren't we a bit far from that? We're living the time of our lives."

"Maybe you are," Ezzy scoffed as he took a swig of his whiskey. "But I'm fucking not. Damn man, sometimes I fucking hate you."

"Okay, low blow and two F-bombs in the same sentence. I wasn't expecting that, bro, I think you've had a bit too much to drink. Let's go, I'll drive you home."

"I ain't going nowhere with you. Mr. Got-It-All-Under-Control. Mr. Money-In-The-Bank. Mr. I'm-Better-Than-You. You think you're a big shot? You're nothing."

"I'm gonna blame it on the alcohol, you're coming with me," Toks said as he grabbed Ezzy's wrist.

"Like hell I am, you sonuvabi--" Ezzy swung at Toks, missed, lost his footing and fell on a table.

Lights out.

CASA DE TOKS

"He's coming to," Toks said.

"Oh thank You, Jesus," Soma whispered.

"He's lucky I didn't introduce them," Toks growled.

Ezzy groaned as he slowly opened his eyes. "Owwwww. What happened?"

"You blacked out," Toks said, reaching for a cup of coffee.

"My head feels like it's got a weight on it."

"That's because it was empty before and now your sense has returned," Soma said curtly. "What did you think you were doing at The Lounge making a fool of yourself?"

Ezzy groaned.

"It's all a blur. The last thing I remember was...Toks...oh shit. I'm sorry, bro. I didn't mean anything I said."

"What did you say?" Soma asked, worried.

"Don't worry about it, Soma, it was nothing. Could you please ask James to brew a fresh pot of coffee?"

"Sure," Soma answered, realizing the men needed some time alone.

"You said some pretty deep things at The Lounge. Wanna talk about it?" Toks asked.

"I'm sorry, bro," Ezzy said, slowly getting off the couch. "I didn't mean any of it."

"I know, man, but there's something eating at you, let's deal with it. I can handle it."

Ezzy took a deep breath and began.

"I just feel like...you know, I feel like I woke up too late. I'm almost forty-five and I don't know why, but it scares the shit out of me. I thought by now, I'd be made. You know, there's all this stuff you're meant to have done by the time you're forty, like own your own home, be financially free, run your own business for a couple of years, and I'm the exact opposite. Worse still, I'm five years behind schedule and don't even look remotely close to achieving any of these goals. I mean, what if nothing pans out even when I'm fifty? Dude, that's five years away! I'm fucking scared. And then I look at you, the poster boy of everything I wanna be but ain't. Forgive me if it sounds like penis envy, but that's how I feel. I mean, how did my life get so screwed up? Where did I get it wrong and how did you get it so damn right?"

"Drink this." Toks poured Ezzy a cup of coffee.

"Talk about getting a load off," Ezzy grinned.

"I know, right?" Toks smiled.

"Dude, seriously, I look at my paycheck from time to time and my take-home pay can barely take me home."

"Then you better change your address."

"Nice one. That's a thought," Ezzy smiled ruefully, sipping his coffee.

"Here's the scoop, bro; first off, your life isn't as screwed up as you think. You've got a wife who loves you, kids who adore you and the respect of your colleagues at work. You've got a decent job, nice crib and you can meet your obligations and for that, you've gotta be grateful."

"I'm grateful, man, but can't I have more?"

"Of course you can, and that's why you're frustrated. Listen, bro, the best I can be to you is a sign that the future you want is possible."

"Oyanow, so how do I live in this future, because I'm tired of my shitty present?"

"First step, drink some coffee." Toks poured him another cup.

"Listen," Toks sighed "I'm not gonna B.S. you. I know exactly what you're going through--"

"Doubt it," Ezzy smirked, sipping on his coffee.

"Better believe it. I went through this exact phase about fifteen years ago. I'd hit rock bottom. Try as I might, nothing worked; I got depressed and was caught up in self-pity. One day, while surfing the internet, I stumbled on an Ad, by some dude who was a Life Strategist, and he was hosting a free seminar. I can never forget the name of the program, Determine Your Destiny."

"Sounds kinda dodgy."

"Well, I thought so too, but hey, like I said, I was already at rock bottom, digging deeper, running outta time and options, but the name resonated with me. So I signed up and showed up for the event. It wasn't a fancy hall, hell, they didn't even have air conditioning; it didn't look like a sold out event, it was just me and probably about 15 other people in all. But I wasn't there for the ambience, I truly needed to get my shit together. Then up walks the guy on the flyer, looked out of place in this shabby hall. I kept wondering what a seemingly successful guy like him was doing in a dump like that and you know how those moments that change your life forever are? Frozen in time; I still remember his topic: Life Is A Week."

"Sounds pretty weak, no pun intended, for a program called Determine Your Destiny," Ezzy scoffed

Toks rolled his eyes and continued: "He began by quoting Psalm 90 verse 12."

"Though you said he was a Life Coach, sounds like a preacher to me."

"That's what I thought at first and I was just about to blank the guy cause me and God weren't on speaking terms, but I figured that if I'd come that far, I might as well hear him out. So he quotes Psalm 90 verse 12 which says...

"...so teach us to number our days, that we may apply our hearts unto wisdom," Ezzy said then burst out laughing at the look on Toks' face. "Don't look all so surprised, man, me and Jesus share the same network provider, I just deyoff my WiFi."

"Just turn on your WiFi, anywhere you dey, e go connect one time. The signal go reach you everywhere you go."

"That one sef dey," Ezzy concurred.

"So this dude reads the scripture," Toks picked up again, "and says that life is like a week of days. Monday is your time between birth to age 10. Tuesday is age 11 - 20, Wednesday is 21 - 30, Thursday is 31 - 40, Friday is 41 - 50."

"Chai, that means I'm in Friday afternoon, shey 44 is afternoon?"

"It would seem so, Saturday is 51 – 60 and Sunday is 61 – 70," Toks finished.

"It's not complete. What if you live beyond 70?"

"That one na public holiday,"Toks said as both men laughed.

"What's so funny?" Soma asked as she and James brought in a pot of coffee and some biscuits. "Is the coast clear? I was half expecting fisticuffs."

"No way, babe," Ezzy said, hugging his wife. "We're good, Toks is sharing some blast from the past ish."

"Don't let me stand in your way, Toks, do continue."

Toks brought Soma up to speed and then continued:

"So, now that we know what time zone each day represents, the next thing is to discover the purpose for each day."

"I was just gonna ask," Ezzy said.

"The Life Strategist then said Monday is the season of Discovery. Since it's the time zone between birth and 10 years old and we're under the guidance of our parents, they, ideally, should be able to observe us as we grow and discover what gifts or talents we exhibit and slowly but surely, train us in the way we were naturally designed to go, so that when we grow up, we won't turn away from that path."

"Why does that sound familiar?" Ezzy quizzed.

"It's in the Bible nah" Soma said, rolling her eyes. "Train up a child in the way he should go, and when he is old, he will not depart from it. Our children learned it as a memory verse in Sunday school."

"At least I knew I'd heard it before. So bro, what happens if you're like me and your parents didn't see all those things because even they had not discovered themselves?"

"That's a good question oh, because I have kids now who are in this time zone and I'm not sure I know what to look out for either. Does that make me a bad parent?" Soma said.

"No, of course not," Toks smiled.

"During the season of discovery, you begin to notice what your children naturally gravitate towards. Our job as parents is to understand what their M.I. is--"

"M.I.? What's Abaga got to do with this?"

"Funny, bro, I don't mean Jude, I'm talking about Multiple Intelligence."

"Ahhhh. Got it. Was wondering what the short black boy had to do with kids, I mean he may be pint-sized and all, but his bars are all grown up."

"Amen to that," Toks grinned. "As I was saying, our job as parents is to understand what our kids' multiple intelligence are. And before you ask, every child is intelligent but wired differently. Some kids are music smart, like 5-year old Michael Jackson and 7-year old Beyonce; some are picture smart, others are word smart; some are nature smart, others, logic smart; some are body smart, these ones often have a flair for sports, like 3-year old Tiger Woods and finally, self smart."

"Self smart definitely sounds like me," Ezzy smiled.

"I doubt it," Toks countered. "People who are self smart are very introspective and reflective; which of course is the very antithesis of who you are."

"Chaiiiiii. 1 - 0. Well done!"

"I think I'm logic smart," Soma said. "I like numbers, chess and complex calculations, my favorite subject was Further Mathematics."

"And I'm the exact opposite, I'm definitely word smart," Toks said.

"So you're saying that as parents to young kids, our job is to determine their multiple intelligence and lead them down that path?"

"Pretty much," Toks said.

"We have to look at Chidi and Bola a lot more seriously," Ezzy said gravely.

"You can say that again," Soma agreed.

"I can hook you up with my friend, Tam Tam."

"What's a Tam Tam?" Ezzy asked mischievously

"She's a friend of mine, Tammy Itam, she's a M.I. expert."

"Is she on Instagram? What's her handle?" Soma asked

"I think it's @tammyitam check her out. Let's get into Tuesday," Toks continued.

"Yes please," Soma agreed. "This is making so much sense."

"Glad to hear it. Now, according to the Life Strategist, Tuesday is the time zone between--"

"11 and 20," Ezzy interjected.

"Glad to see you're paying attention," Toks smirked "And as Ezzy has so eloquently described, Tuesday is the time zone between 11 and 20 years old and this is the season of Practice."

"You're welcome," Ezzy said, raising a glass.

"In your Tuesday, this is the point where you hone your skills and begin to develop the work ethic and the hours that deliver consistent performance."

"Like Malcolm Gladwell's 10,000-hour rule," Soma said.

"Exactly!" Toks said.

"Malcolm who?" asked Ezzy.

"Malcolm Gladwell," Toks replied.

"Wasn't he in prison in the 60's for being a Black Panther or something?"

"Nah man, that was Malcolm X and no, he wasn't a Black Panther."

"But the movie was the ish!!! As in, Marvel killed it! Almost as good as Avengers Endgame."

"Here's to Tony Stark for saving us all," Toks said, lifting his glass.

"To Iron Man. I love you 3000," Ezzy said, raising his glass and taking a sip of wine.

"Oya oh, if you two have finished gisting about a 3 billion dollar movie, then we can get back to helping me discover my own billions."

"True that. Let's stay on message. So Tuesday is the season of practice. But here's the challenge, how can you practice what you've not yet discovered?"

"Word."

"If you don't mind me using a Biblical reference, David wasn't even old enough to join the army to fight Goliath and when Saul tried to talk him out of it because of his youth, David told Saul that facing opposition like Goliath wasn't his first rodeo and then talked about his past experience of having practiced with the lion and bear."

"That's true."

"I mean, check it out. The Williams sisters were barely teenagers when they burst on the scene, but they'd been practicing since they were barely 6 years old, and now they're in their 30's and champions."

"Makes sense," Ezzy mused. "They've had over 25 years of constant performance."

"You got it, bro! And you took me right to my next point. Wednesday, the season of Performance. But here's the conundrum. How can you practice what you've not discovered?"

"Oro jade," Ezzy said.

"Ase tele," Soma responded.

"O deep abi?" Toks grinned "That's the whole idea, guys. Wednesday is the time zone between 21 and 30 and it's the season of performance. In this season, you begin to display on a much larger stage, all you've practiced in your Tuesday."

"I can imagine. Look at all these footballers; see Neymar nah. Shey he's the world's most expensive player and how old is he sef? 26! Just 26? See Pogba, he's 25," Ezzy remarked.

"It's not just in sports, look at music and entertainment; Rihanna is 29 and she's been at this for what seems to be forever," Soma added.

"It only seems like that because they woke up on the right day at the right time," Toks replied.

"That's deep," Soma said "They woke up on the right day at the right time."

"Absolutely, Neymar and Pogba woke up on the right day, Monday and at the right time to discover what their gifts were; practiced on their Tuesday, putting in the work and building the ethic, failing sometimes, until time and chance collided and they're now performing in their Wednesday."

"Unlike some of us, that didn't wake up until Thursday morning and now realize we have a heck of a lot of catching up to do," Ezzy said ruefully.

"Perhaps, but the person that wakes up at 3pm will have a greater sense of urgency than the one who woke up at 3am."

"True that, bro. It's time to get our hustle on."

"But here's the interesting thing, you can actually be several seasons ahead your age."

"How do you mean?" Soma asked.

"Well, let's use Neymar, Pogba and Rihanna. They're not just not in the season of performance, they're living their Thursday, even though they're in the Wednesday time zone."

"You lost me, bro, bring it back," Ezzy said.

"Okay, let me try again. Neymar, Pogba and Rihanna are in their 20s, which would put them in their Wednesday, yeah?"

"Yeah, so far so good," Ezzy replied.

"But these guys aren't just performers on the world stage, they're masters."

"Guarandamnteed!" Soma chuckled, "I've always wanted to say it since I heard it for the first time."

"Mastery is the next season, which is the time zone between 31 and 40 and it's your Thursday. So what I'm saying is they're experiencing Thursday season while still in their Wednesday. Capisce?"

"Capisce!"

"In the season of Mastery, as implied, you've already become a master at your craft and should be regarded as a name reference or industry leader, where your name defines your niche."

"See my life!" Ezzy moaned. "15 years in Advertising and I'll be lucky if I'm a footnote in the chronicles of my company, let's forget about being a name in the industry."

"It's okay, bro, we're all wiser with the benefit of hindsight."

"Yeah," Ezzy said wryly. "But shit just got real. I mean, how can you master what you have not performed; how can you perform what you've not practiced and how can you practice what you've not discovered?"

"By starting now," Toks answered, placing a sympathetic hand on his friend's shoulder.

"Yeah, we're Team 3PM. We started late, but we're gonna make every minute count," Soma said, hugging her husband.

"You guys sure I shouldn't tell James to hook you up with the guest suite?" Toks grinned.

"Ooooh Toks, we're fine," Soma said, blushing.

"If you insist. Okay, moving on. So we're done with Monday through to Thursday, now we're about to wind down for the weekend, starting with Friday."

"Definitely my favorite day of the week," said Ezzy.

"So Friday is the time zone between 41 and 50."

"I'll take that back. Na Friday morning I dey so. Shey 44 is still morning?"

"Yep. You and I are about the same age, aren't we?" Toks asked

"Ehn, I use 6 months senior you, but you use maybe six billion naira senior me." Ezzy laughed.

"Very funny, bro. Anyways, Friday is the season of Mentoring and

Multiplication."

"I like the sound of that - M and M. It's got a nice to ring to it," Soma said.

"Especially when it's mixed with Coldstone ice cream, sonuva—"

"Moving on, people!" Toks interrupted. "So Friday is the season of--"

"M and M!" Ezzy and Soma yelled enthusiastically as they high-fived each other.

"You guys are so shameless. How old are you? 12?"

"13 next month," Ezzy said, smiling.

"Joker. So Friday is the season of--, never mind, I'm not falling for that twice. In this season, being a master in your field, you now step up to a higher level - Coaching; where you begin to express your value in not only mentoring others, but in multiplying systems that help others discover, practice, perform and ultimately master themselves as you take them through this value chain."

"Makes sense. That's the football academy model. So football clubs invest in discovering next generation talent, create an environment for them to practice, and give them opportunities to perform as they ultimately become masters of their craft as the cycle continues." Ezzy said.

"Exactly! Still staying with your football analogy, Monday, you're a recruit, playing in the Little League, Tuesday you're playing in the Under 18's, Wednesday you're playing in the Premiership or La Liga, Thursday you're World Footballer of the Year, Friday you're a Coach."

"I love it," Soma said. "I mean, some of the football-speak was gibberish to me but I understood the trend. It's all about transition."

"Exactly, Soma. Now imagine someone in Monday trying to be a Coach in their Friday."

"Abeg, which experience does he have?"

"Now imagine someone who should be a Coach playing in the Little League."

"Agbaya, his time has passed."

"Exactly! So there are certain seasons you must leverage because they are fleeting and once you've missed out on, you can't ever get back and in the same vein, there are certain seasons you don't qualify for, simply because you haven't gotten enough experiences or results yet, so we must all understand our seasons."

"So what about Saturday and Sunday," Soma asked.

"Great question. But first off, I must say this: You have no business working on the weekend."

"Hmm. Word. That's some deep ish right there!"

"Tweetable! I've got to write that down" Soma said as she reached for her trusty notepad. "You have no business working on the weekend.

"That's deep," she reiterated.

"Yeah, think about it. You go to an office or a bank and who's there to open the gate for you? A security man, or in this case, a gateman. As far as I'm concerned we have more gatemen than security guards; but I digress. Here's my point, many of these gatemen are elderly folks who sadly are past their prime, who aren't working because they're passionate about security. They're not working because they want to, they're working because they have to.

"Nobody ever says they wanna end up a gateman in future, it happens because they kept their eyes on the present and didn't give the future much thought. Listen guys, most talents are time-bound, meant to be maximized at the peak of your strength, because someday, diminishing returns will set in. You have no business working on the weekend. And if you do have to work, work because you want to, not because you have to. So allow me to put it in perspective, Saturday and Sunday are the time zones between 51 and 60, and 61 and 70 respectively. Saturday is the season of Recreation while Sunday is the season of Rest."

"Rest in peace tinz," Ezzy said.

"Not exactly, but let me take it a step at a time. Saturday is the season of recreation."

"Won't we be too old for fun and games at 60?" Ezzy asked.

"Not that kind of recreation. I mean re - creation, to create oneself afresh. Pretty much rebranding."

"Aah, now I get it."

"Great. So in this season, you've carved a niche as a master in your craft, here, you've gotta become more strategic. So you'll see that for over 25 years, Oprah was identified as The Queen of Talk, but she recreated herself from being a talk show host and became a TV Network owner. She still gets to be in the same field, but now she's playing at a much higher strategic level."

"Not to mention, more profitable," Ezzy added.

"Bill Gates did the same thing. He resigned as CEO of Microsoft, then became Chief Software Engineer, but that still wasn't it for him, then he followed his passion for philanthropy and solving global problems and started the Bill and Melinda Gates Foundation," Soma said.

"Absolutely, Soma. He's recreated himself and that always gives renewed vigor to pursue new interests."

"Not to mention live longer," Ezzy said, sipping his drink.

Toks nodded in agreement, then continued. "Which now dovetails into Sunday, the season of rest."

"--in peace," Ezzy quipped.

"Nope. Rejuvenation. It's rest and rejuvenation, where your youth is restored."

"Probably by popping some of those little blue pills."

"Speak for yourself, bro. But in the time zone of 61 to 70, you're resting from your labors and can actually enjoy your life in relative comfort, surrounded by what really matters--"

"Lots of money?" Ezzy interrupted, grinning.

"No. Family," Soma said, as she pinched her husband on the thigh.

"Owww! Owww! Owwww!"

TOTAL MONEY WORKOUT

1. What day of the week are you?
2. What season of life are you currently on?
3. What can you do to speed up your season?

CHAPTER TEN

THE WHEEL OF WEALTH

Secret 10: Wealth is a wheel that if you spin fast enough, it will end up carrying you

Hassan slumped in his chair and muttered under his breath.

"Man, Ezzy, I don't know about you o, but with all this work we dey so, e be like say monkey dey work and na baboon dey chop."

"Wetin happen, bros?"Ezzy asked. Frustration was evident in his friend's voice.

"Dude, the shit is gradually gonna hit the proverbial fan. I mean, I've had it up to here. This recession ain't funny, man. You remember I told you some time back that I've been up to my ears in bills."

"Yeah, you mentioned sorting out some of your folks' outstanding bills as well some other stuff."

"Dude," Hassan continued, "Just when I thought it couldn't get worse, the bottom fell out of the barrel."

"What happened?" Ezzy groaned. He silently hoped that Hassan wasn't about to ask him for money because he didn't have any to spare. His Total Money Workout plan was like a well regimented workout, with Toks as his eagle-eyed and merciless gym instructor.

"This country won't succeed in killing me. I feel Naija has put me on its hit list and is out to get me, cause everywhere I go, somebody, somewhere is taking potshots at me. You know that we've been on this job for a while, so I've been trying to improve my career options, so last year, I enrolled in a Masters Degree online program with one of those universities wey dey Jand."

"Error...," Ezzy groaned, he could see the end of this story from a mile away.

"Guy, na so I come enroll for this course o. I dey do 'pay as you go', I sha suppose pay in six installments. Ezzy, wallahi, when I started this course, 1 Pound na 250 Naira. Bros, three installments to go, now wey person don reach half way mark, we come enter recession; now, 1 Mama Charlie don reach 600 Naira!"

"Chaiiiii!" exclaimed Ezzy.

"Guy, I for say I dey poor like church rat, but you sef know say na church rat dey flex pass."

"As in," Ezzy laughed.

"Guy, no dey play," Hassan slapped Ezzy on his head. "Wetin man go do?"

"E be like say na to take loan from church rat be dat."

CASA DE TOKS

7.15 pm

"Hey guys. Great to see you again. Sorry about the short notice," Toks said as he welcomed Ezzy and Soma into his sprawling living room and signaled to his butler.

"James, could you please bring some refreshments for my guests?"

"Of course, sir," the butler bowed as he turned to leave.

"Toks, you really need to hook me up with one of these butlers, man," Ezzy said as he slumped into a leather sofa.

"Not until we're financially fit. Toks, don't mind him," Soma retorted.

"Sorry, bro, I gotta listen to your wife's wise words," Toks grinned.

"I couldn't agree more," Ezzy said. "Truly, Toks, this Total Money Workout journey has really changed my thinking and habits in relation to making, managing and mastering money."

"Absolutely, Toks. I feel a lot leaner, trimmer and healthier. It's almost like the physical workouts I have with my Health Coach, Remi Owadokun. Ruthless, intense, but eventually a lifestyle change full of results," Soma concurred.

"I'm sure Remi would be glad to hear that," Toks grinned as he led them into his study.

"So, now that you guys have mastered the basics, it's time for the advanced lesson," he continued.

"Advanced? Dude, I thought we were on Easy Street now," Ezzy groaned, rolling his eyes.

Soma squeezed her husband's hand reassuringly. "Don't worry, babe, I've got you. We're a team."

Ezzy smiled at his wife. This journey of financial fitness had made them much closer than they had been since their first year of marriage. He wondered how many homes had collapsed under the strain from a series of poor financial decisions, poverty stress and not understanding their money mentalities.

"Yeah, babe, we're a team," he smiled, running his fingers through his wife's hair.

"Oh, not the hair. I just had it done," Soma groaned, brushing him away, playfully.

"If you two love birds would like a room, that guest suite offer is still open o," Toks said cheekily.

"No thanks, Toks, we're fine," blushed Soma.

"What she's trying to say is no thanks, we've already had lunch, if you know what I mean," Ezzy winked as Soma punched him on the arm.

"Glad to hear it," Toks grinned.

"So, to the matter at hand. I wanted to discuss your Wheel of Wealth."

"Oooh...I like the sound of that," Soma said as she reached for her trusty notepad. "Yup, I'm ready, go on, Toks."

Toks reached for his markers and drew a circle on his white board.

"Let's get to it," he said. "I like to think of wealth as a wheel, with each of its spokes defining a specific category."

"I'm curious to know what the spokes are," Ezzy said as the butler set the refreshments on the coffee table.

'I'll tell you," Toks continued. "There are eight dimensions of wealth and they are Income, Savings, Investments, Wealth Creation, Land and Real Estate, Debt Elimination, Insurance and Charitable Giving."

"I can already tell I'm far from wealthy even if I look wealthy from afar," Ezzy moaned.

"Wow! That's a tweetable!" exclaimed Soma as she wrote down Ezzy's words.*"A lot of people are far from wealthy even if though they look wealthy from afar."*

"That's deep, honey." She smiled.

"That's how I roll," Ezzy grinned. "I'm a poet and I don't know it, I'm so deep I'm underground."

"That's why your rap career never got off the ground," Toks retorted.

"Haaaaa! Dude, you just scored. Nice one. 1 – 0." Ezzy clapped.

Soma rolled her eyes as she watched the two men.

"Oya Kid and Play, can we get back to some serious business?"

"Niiicceee, did you see what she did right there?" Ezzy said, clapping.

"Babe, I didn't know you were a rap head too, how come you know Kid and Play?"he asked.

"You think that because I'm a wife and mother now, that I don't have game? Leave story, I'll tell you later," Soma grinned. "Toks, please carry on. I'm interested in knowing more about the Wheel of Wealth."

"Ah yes. Where was I?" Toks asked.

"The eight dimensions of wealth," Soma replied.

"Absolutely. But let me give a caveat, I'm speaking of wealth from the platform of money. I realize that wealth is not limited to what you have in your bank account. You can be lacking in finances, but rich in health or your family relationships. That's not the context from which I'm speaking. Right now, I'm dealing with wealth from the financial perspective alone. Capisce?"

"Yes, Godfather," Ezzy and Soma replied in unison.

"Jinx!" They exclaimed at the same time as they laughed.

Toks smiled, casting his mind back to how fractious their marriage was before he got involved in coaching them. *Definitely the best part of my job*, he thought.

"Okay, lovebirds, settle down. The offer still stands if you want James to open up the Guest suite for you," he winked.

Soma pushed her husband away, blushing.

"Now that we're on the same page, let's get to it. The first dimension of the Wheel of Wealth is Income. And as you know, this is money earned from your direct earnings, technically what I call sweat-related earnings or fondly known as your salary. This is the lowest rung on the ladder of wealth. Wealth requires a foundation to be built, and many times, it begins with your income. Now, I know you're gonna say that your income isn't enough--"

"My thoughts exactly," Ezzy interjected.

"But here's my point," Toks continued. "It's not what you don't have that limits you, it's what you have, but don't know how to use."

"Tweetable!" Soma yelled as she scribbled Toks' words in her notebook.

"It's not what you don't have that limits you, it's what you have, but don't know how to use."

Toks continued.

"What you do with your income is determined by your most dominant thoughts, and most times, these thoughts are more *present-based* than *future-focused.*"

"Hmmm... Go on," Ezzy said.

"Think about it this way, do you remember what your budget or spending plan looked like before we started our Total Money Workout coaching sessions? Over 90% of your income was dedicated to paying off bills that were in your present, like your NEPA or what do they call it now, PHCN bill, your DSTV bill, your in laws and outlaws, fuel, transportation and all what not. All these bills barely allowed you or left you with anything to be future focused, simply because your dominant thought was survival. Even though your heart longed for success, your actions followed the path of survival."

"That's true," Soma concurred. "We were so broke that I became such a penny-pinching *frugalista,*" she said, blushing.

"Yeah, it was worrying about our bills that had me drinking at The Lounge the day we met, piling up more bills," Ezzy reminisced.

"Luckily, you only chose to drown your sorrows in a few beers, sadly, many others driven down this path have drowned more than their sorrows."

"True," Ezzy said, raising a glass. "We're just one of the lucky ones."

"So Toks, you're saying that in order to build wealth, it's more of a future, long term game, right?" Soma asked.

"That's right. You can't earn your way to a fortune. You have to make money your slave. So let's get to the second dimension on the Wheel of Wealth - Savings. Now your savings by themselves, can't in any way make you wealthy. And as you've already learned from the SIT plan, your savings are for short term projects. Now, you shouldn't be saving for the sake of it, your savings goals should be to lead you to the third dimension on your Wheel of Wealth, investments. But let's not get ahead of ourselves, let's focus on the Savings dimension. Now, I'm all for growing your nest egg, but again, it's all about intention."

"How so?" Ezzy asked.

"Well, are you saving to save or to invest?"

"What's the difference?" Soma asked.

"Okay, since I've previously covered savings, using the SIT principle, let's jump ahead to the third dimension on the Wheel of Wealth, *Investments*, so I can answer your question by tying these concepts together. The difference between investing and saving is really quite simple. It's the risk factor. Most people save money in financial instruments such as savings accounts where they can earn some interest, simply because there's no risk. Investments on the other hand, always have some element of risk. You know the saying, *no risk, no reward.* So, savings means keeping aside some part of your income, while investments means keeping some of that money in financial products to earn returns and grow your portfolio. The second major difference is access to your funds or what they call liquidity. Your savings are the most liquid, which simply means they can be accessed anytime, while investments aren't so easy to access. So here's my big idea, if you are going to need the money in the near future, save it. If you aren't going to touch the money for a longer time frame, invest it."

"That's a relief," Ezzy said. "But what do I invest in?"

"That's a tough one," Toks replied, pouring himself a stiff drink.

"Now, while I really can't tell you where to keep your money, you might wanna consult an investment banker for that, but I will say this. Here's my

Golden Rule of investing: Investigate before you invest."

"Hmmm. That's deep!" Ezzy exclaimed.

"Tweetable!" Soma smiled as she scribbled furiously into her notepad. *"Investigate before you invest."*

"Dude, how do you come up with these insights?"

"The bitter pill of experience, bro. I wish I could say otherwise, but that's the truth. I remember many years ago, I'd saved a good chunk of my income and was looking for what to invest in. A friend of mine and I saw opportunities in Agriculture and decided to open a farm. To be honest, we were lured by projections and smooth talking con men who didn't have the track record--"

"Sorry to cut you off, Toks," said Soma. "So are you saying that anyone who's asking you to invest in something must have also invested in it?"

"That's my thinking. I believe that if someone's encouraging you to take advantage of an investment opportunity, he ain't Santa Claus brimming with the milk of human kindness and decided to bless you with a present; it stands to reason that he should've also put his money where his mouth is. If it's such a great opportunity – and you must have proof, don't be lured by smooth talkers – ask them to show you their returns and their portfolio over a six to nine-month period."

"That makes sense," Soma concurred.

"So, we invested well over six million bucks into this farm and in a year, lost all our money because we trusted blindly, simply because our investment was in a part of the country that we couldn't monitor."

"Pheeewwww," whistled Ezzy.

"Six M! That's not beans."

"Tell me about it," Toks said as he sipped his drink. "That also taught me an important lesson. Trust, but verify."

"Tweetable!" yelled Soma as she scribbled in her trusty notepad.

"Trust, but verify."

"Toks, why you no tell me dis thing since nah? Chai, I for don hear word. I've learned that lesson the hard way."

"What happened?" Toks asked, furrowing his brow.

Ezzy continued, visibly embarrassed. "That's how I just enter one chance with MMM."

"Ehn? MM gini?" Soma asked, doing a double take.

"Babe, I can explain," Ezzy replied, scratching his head.

"You better start explaining. Come oh, I hope you didn't touch the kids' school fees? Me and you will just enter the same trouser. I can't believe you still went on with it, after I warned you not to get caught up with this MMM buzz..."

"You guys talked about it?" Toks asked.

"Yeah, we did," Ezzy replied, wryly

"So why did you go ahead?" Soma asked, raising her voice several decibels higher.

"I don't know. I guess I got caught up with the buzz. I mean, Hassan from the office had some issues and needed to raise some money for his online MBA programme...he put three hundred thousand and got six hundred thousand...I wouldn't have believed it if I hadn't seen it with my own eyes.. And I thought of how it would be nice to have some extra cash for a change. I mean, our Total Money Workout programme has leaned us out, helped us cut out unnecessary spending habits--"

"Not all of them, I see," muttered Toks under his breath.

"Ooohhh, I'm already feeling like an idiot, don't rub it in."

"Don't rub it in?" Soma yelled. "See this guy oh. You haven't seen anything yet. So how much of our money did you put into MMM?"

Ezzy shuffled his feet along Toks' parquet floor.

"Chai. I don die--"

"Ezekiel, you're already dead, so you better talk," Soma growled.

"When I saw how much Hassan made, I mean, he got N600k! That's N300k profit on his investment! And then, once that worked, he was willing to drop another five hundred..."

"Jesus, I'm finished," Soma held her head in her hands.

"I said if I can get one million naira, since I was due to collect our monthly contribution in the office..."

"Yeee! Mogbe!" Soma exclaimed.

"So Hassan and I put in N500k--"

"Please tell me that was N250k each," Toks asked.

"No..." Ezzy said, sheepishly. "N500k each. I pulled the money from our savings."

"Mo ku!" Soma pulled off her scarf.

"And how much did you guys lose?" Toks asked.

"Everything," Ezzy moaned.

"Mo da ron," Soma screamed as she reached for her fleet-footed husband.

"Now, I know what MMM means," Toks said, reaching for his drink. "Mogbe. Moku. Modaron."

An hour later, after Toks had restrained Soma from hurling several choice invectives and a few expensive objects at her significantly bruised husband, they continued their conversation.

"Mtsscheew!" Soma hissed. "Onuku. Anu ofia."

"I don't understand Igbo, but I know you're abusing me," Ezzy growled.

"Before nko? Shouldn't I do more than that? You're lucky that Toks is here and we're not at home, you won't have heard the last of it."

"At this rate, it might be the last thing I ever hear," Ezzy said sarcastically.

"What did you say?" Soma asked, trying to slap her husband again.

"That would be enough from both of you," Toks bellowed. "Come on guys, what's done is done. Ezzy, what you did was irresponsible and selfish--"

"Tell him!" Soma hissed.

"And Soma, I would appreciate it if you didn't try to deliberately become a widow, prematurely."

"Sorry, man."

"I'm sorry, Toks" Soma echoed.

"Listen guys, I understand your frustration. You're not the first to fall for a Ponzi scheme. Now Ezzy, if you want to be absolutely one hundred with me, you'll admit that your motives may have been a tad selfish and not entirely altruistic."

"Well, I saw Hassan's returns...It seemed too good to be true."

"If it's too good to be true, it's usually a lie."

"Shey you see? But Toks," interjected Soma "what about Network Marketing or MLM?"

"That one na the real scam," Ezzy scoffed.

"Not particularly," Toks replied.

"Now, do I think that most Network Marketing salesmen omit the fine print and gloss over the benefits? Absolutely. Look guys, I'm not gonna fool you. Creating passive income takes a heck of a lot of active work. The idea that you're gonna sit on the beach and do nothing while your money's toiling for you isn't as easy as it sounds. There's a heck of a lot of work that goes into it. Unfortunately, we're so blinded by the projections and have built estates in the air and fail to realize that once you're done dreaming, it's time to rise and grind.

That's why when folks realize they've gotta do a lot of work convincing others to sell their products and join their down lines or whatever, they realize it's not that easy. They realize they have to face their own insecurities and limiting beliefs if they have to sell a product to a complete stranger; they get overwhelmed and eventually, forfeit their initial investment, which ultimately benefits the Network Marketing company. Besides, it's called Network MARKETING, not Network Chilling. Sadly, too many people are looking for ways to beat the system, and like gamblers in Vegas casinos, they're blinded by the bright lights and dulled by the booze, and because they're having many near wins, they keep going; unfortunately, they forget the cardinal rule. The house always wins."

"Tell me about it," Ezzy groaned. "The house always wins."

"Toks, now that my dearly departing, sorry, beloved husband has lost his salary, I think we need to quickly move to the next spoke on the Wheel of Wealth, Wealth Creation."

"Great idea, Soma. So Wealth Creation is an incredible tool to build wealth. I mean, you literally can't become wealthy if you don't understand the principles of creating wealth. We've already established that your job gives you income, which is the first rung on your ladder of wealth, but it's not sufficient to grow your wealth, because it requires your being present to grow your income. To grow your wealth, you require a business platform or side hustle, since you're in employment."

"But Toks, do you think everyone's wired to be an entrepreneur, or should everyone start a business?"

"No, Soma, I don't think so. Some folk have entrepreneurship wired in their DNA, they probably were natural born salesmen, selling things while they were kids, while some others recognize an opportunity and provide a solution which then creates an awareness in their minds as they find their path along the way. Entrepreneurship is a mentality. It's a mentality that does not accept the limitations of a salary. It says you don't get to determine how much I make. It says while my salary can determine how much you're going to pay me, but you can't determine how much I'm going to make. Because how much I'm going to make is only determined by the tenacity of my own creativity. So, to answer your question, Soma, not everyone can be an entrepreneur because it requires a substantial appetite for risk. I mean, it involves overcoming inertia, launching, raising capital, facing and handling rejection from investors and customers alike...it can be pretty daunting. So most folk would rather avoid the disruption that comes with being an entrepreneur and have the certainty of a comfortable job, with predictable schedules and a regular paycheck."

"You're preaching to the choir," Soma said. "I'm so risk averse."

"Why do you think that is?" Toks asked.

Soma closed her eyes firmly and began tapping her pencil on her notepad.

"You don't have to talk about it if it's too painful for you," Toks demurred.

"Babe, are you okay?" Ezzy asked, taking a careful step towards her; his ears were still ringing from the slap she had given him earlier.

Soma took a deep breath and began to speak.

"My dad had a full time job, working at an oil and gas firm and our lives were to die for. We were chauffeur-driven, to and from school; we travelled abroad on every summer holiday and we were the envy of our friends and neighbors. I mean, we were living a charmed life--"

"I didn't know that," Ezzy said.

"I've been so ashamed about who or what we used to be."

"So what changed?" Ezzy asked

"He was downsized or I think the politically correct term is right sized. Anyway, he sha lost his job. The company gave him a severance cheque which at that time was worth a lot of money, so my dad, looking for ways to grow his fast depleting income, invested in a haulage business. To be fair, he really didn't know the first or last thing about haulage, I guess he just wanted to have something that was his, after all, he'd worked for eighteen years, only to realize the job he'd poured his life into wasn't even his to keep. Sha, long story short, my dad sunk all his severance pay into that business, got gyped by a few unsavory characters, inevitably had a stroke and died."

"Baby, I'm sorry..."

"It's fine. I'm sorry I never told you how my dad died. Luckily for us, he had a lot of goodwill, so a few friends of his became responsible for our upkeep and education. I guess that's why each time Ezzy brings up some business idea, I'm quick to shoot it down, simply because I'm afraid that what happened with my dad will repeat itself and I can't imagine having the kids going through what I did."

Ezzy sighed as he hugged his wife tighter.

"That's quite an incredible story, Soma," Toks said. "Thank God we don't look like what we've been through."

"Amen to that," Ezzy concurred as he waved his hand in the air.

"I'm sorry about your dad. Unfortunately, it takes more than being a good person to succeed in business and for some weird reason, good people seem to be pretty bad at business. Now, that's not to imply that all good business men are bad people either, I mean, I'm relatively successful at business and I dare say I'm a pretty standup guy, but it's just that business usually requires a lot of pragmatism and little or no emotional decisions. I mean, from what you say, your dad obviously was a good man and probably good at his job, but the company probably made a judgment call based on their bottom line and business realities. Did they know that a lot of people's lives would be upturned? Absolutely! Was it their concern if those people were inadequately prepared for what life was going to throw at them next? Probably not. Why? Because personal development is personal. Here's my big idea, guys. Your 9 to 5 will move you forward in life, but your 5 to 9 will move you upward in life."

"Tweetable!" Soma cheered lightly as she scribbled Toks' words into her notepad.

"Your 9 to 5 will move you forward in life, but your 5 to 9 will move you upward in life."

"You need to leverage your *9 to 5* to build capacity for your *5 to 9*. Go to work, earn a great living, but when you get home, don't turn on the television just yet, take a shower and get into your hustle wear. If you work as hard on your hustle as you do on your job, you'll be firing on all cylinders and the process of wealth creation will begin."

"Man, I need to get me some hustle wear," Ezzy grinned.

"Dude, all your clothes are hustle wear," Toks smiled.

"Nice one. 2 - 0."

"Soma, so now you see that the reason you're so business averse is simply tied to your life experiences."

"True. So how do I change that?"

"Well, you have to associate a new response to your past experience."

"Hmm... associate a new response to your past experience,"Soma repeated.

"Definitely sounds like a tweetable," Ezzy grinned.

"I think so too," Soma agreed as she scribbled in her notebook.

"I'll explain. Think about life as an equation; I + R = O where I is the influence, which many times is external; R is your response and O is the outcome or experience. Now, in this equation, there are two constants, which are the influence and the outcome. The only variable is your response and that's within your control. So when something happens to you from either an internal or external influence, your response to that influence will ultimately determine the outcome, which inevitably becomes your life experience. So, when your dad lost his job, business and money, that was the Influence; the response you attached to that scenario was that going into business makes people lose money and the outcome is that they eventually lose their lives."

"Hmmm...that's true," concurred Soma.

"So, in order to change your experience about business, you must be willing to associate a new response to it."

"Easier said than done, I'm sure. Okay, how do I do that?"

"Simple. So you associated business failure with your dad, now when you think of business, you think failure. Now, do the opposite. Who can you associate business success with? Who do you know that has succeeded in business?"

"That's not rocket science...you!" Soma grinned.

"That's very kind of you to say. Okay, let's proceed. The easiest way to delete an old program is to create and repeat a new one. Now, in order to do that, we've got to create new neural pathways..."

"Neural pathways? E be like say we don enter science class be dat," Ezzy said, scratching his head.

"Don't worry, it's not that complicated. Neurons are nerve cells that transmit signals to and from the brain; and the neural pathway is the route through which information passes from one neuron to the next."

"Still not making this science class easier," Ezzy yawned.

"Okay, let me try the *Science for Dummies* version," Toks grinned.

"Much better," Ezzy smiled, giving a thumbs up.

"Let's think of two neurons as two locations, say Lekki and Ikeja. The neural pathway is the road that leads to them. How am I doing so far?"

"So far, so good."

"So the more times you drive on the road, the more solid the road becomes and the more familiar you are with the road, Capisce?"

"Capisce, Godfather. I understand."

"And the reverse is true. The less times you drive along that road, the more fragile the road and the less familiar it becomes."

"Hmmm...that makes sense," Soma murmured.

"So are you saying that as long as I don't drive along the road of business failure and focus on driving along the road of business success, my fear of business failure will naturally fall away?"

"Soma, I don't think I could have said it any better. Let me add one more thing. Focus creates blindness. Give an example. If I'm looking at the beach front, can I see the TV behind me?"

"No," Soma replied.

"That's the power of focus. As long as I'm focused on success, I don't notice failure as much. It doesn't mean it's not there. It just means it doesn't have my focus. You empower what you focus on, so you've gotta know what to be focused on and what to be blind to."

"That's a tweetable right there. *You've gotta know what to be focused on and what to be blind to.*"

"Too many people are focused on what they should be blind to and blind to what they should be focused on," Toks continued.

"Damn!" Ezzy screamed. "Toks you be killing it like MI murdered Vector on that *Viper* diss track."

"Dude, Vector's career was already in a coma, and when he went for MI with his diss track, there were some signs of life, but man, MI turned off the life support machine," Toks laughed as he fist-bumped his friend.

"See these agbayas," Soma chuckled. "You don't know you guys are old."

"Soma, leave that thing. You're only as old as you feel, ask RMD and Denzel."

"My boo and bae respectively," Soma clapped.

"Abeggiii, Toks what's the next spoke on the Wheel of Wealth?"

"Can't compete with RMD and Denzel ba?" Toks chuckled.

"Bros, who can? Abeg, make them stay for their lane."

"Preach. Anyway, let's get on to the next spoke on our wheel; and it's one that most folks take for granted, or believe is out of their reach, it's Land and Real Estate."

"Dude, that one sef na scam central. That's how one guy will just print fliers and say he's developing an estate in Mowe or Agbara or some far-flung location, that he's sure you can't make a trip to, or if you can, take you to someone else's property and then collect money from plenty people and eventually cash out," Ezzy scoffed.

"Perhaps. But like I've said before, investigate before you invest. But beyond the risks involved, I'm a big believer that land, in and of itself, is not an asset."

"Toks, I don't understand. I thought you said that land is on the Wheel of Wealth?"

"And I did, Soma, but stay with me, there's a method to my madness. Most folks buy land and keep it, in the hopes of it appreciating in value, which it ultimately does, over a period of time; but that value in appreciation is mostly predicated by the rate of development. So they're playing the long game of value appreciation over time. But remember what our definition of an asset is?"

"Anything that puts money into your pocket," Soma replied.

"Absolutely. So in my opinion, land that isn't earning for you isn't an asset, especially because you can't flip it over quickly if you wanted to get a buyer."

"But Toks, I've always been told that land is an asset," Soma said.

"I've heard that spiel too. But let me prove my argument. Are all lands assets? Can all land be flipped over for a profit? Let me put this in perspective. Imagine the states ravaged by the violence fostered by Boko Haram. I'm certain that before terrorism reared its ugly head in Borno state, there was regular trade and commerce. People owned land and real estate. But guess what? All of a sudden, the city became a hotbed of terror, lives were lost and many people fled the villages and cities. Did property values rise or fall? Didn' those assets lose their value? Would you be willing to buy land and property ir

Borno state for example, even though you could probably get them for next to nothing now?"

"Lai lai oh. Okay, I'll bite for a second," Ezzy said, unconvinced "So how do you turn land into an asset?"

"Simple. You get the land to earn its value for you."

Soma and Ezzy still looked puzzled, so Toks continued.

"Most people keep land indefinitely, hoping to be able to raise enough money to start developing the property, so they can be free of landlords and paying rent."

"Baba God, answer my prayer. Free me from my blood-sucking landlord," Ezzy said.

"From your mouth to God's ear," Toks smiled.

"As I said, I'm a big believer in getting your land to earn its value, so let me explain. Assume I bought a plot of land in Agbara for a million bucks--"

"Big boy!" Ezzy clapped, "land never reach 1M for that side."

"It's only an example, man. So, assuming I bought a plot of land in Agbara for a million bucks, conventional wisdom suggests that I leave it to lie fallow until I raise enough capital to clear it, fence it and possibly get my permit from the State Government--"

"Dude, that one na long thing," Ezzy interrupted, shaking his head.

"I agree. So instead of waiting for a forward-thinking administration to drive development to my forgotten neck of the woods, I would put something on the land that could generate a million bucks. For example, I might decide that since the land already grows stuff, I'd be more deliberate about what grows on it. So I'll start a small farm to grow vegetables, like cassava, which could be processed into garri, which could eventually be sold, or with the right experienced hands, start a micro fish pond all from my little piece of land."

"Hmm...true talk."

"That's true. You can literally get the land to pay for itself and the money you get from it can be used to build the foundations of your real estate empire."

"Absolutely, Soma, it's all about deliberate focus. There's a scripture in Genesis 1:11 that resonates with me so well, and it says:

"Then God said, let the earth bring forth grass, the herb yielding seed, and the fruit tree yielding its fruit after its kind, whose seed is in itself, upon the earth and it was so."

Ezzy and Soma looked perplexed.

"Still don't get the Bible study, bro," shrugged Ezzy.

"I kinda figured. Everything God made had the ability to reproduce according to its kind, probably not big news--"

"Nah, not quite." Ezzy grinned.

"Perhaps, but the clincher is that the seed of everything is in itself. Check it out guys. The seed of humanity is in humans. The seed of trees are in their fruit, so the seed of property is in the land, and the seed of real estate is in the house, the seed of the house is in the rent...the seed of the greater is always in the lesser. The seed for what you want is in what you have!"

"Damn! Oro! That's definitely a tweetable," Ezzy exclaimed.

"*The seed for what you want is in what you have,*" Soma scribbled into her notebook.

"You're feeling it, right?" Toks said, excitedly.

"So remember like I said before, when it comes to building real estate, don't just build a home to live in, especially now that you understand that the seed of an estate is in the house, my recommendation is to build real estate that you can rent out in order to give you seeds to build more property."

"Makes sense, man," Ezzy concurred.

"So going back to our Wheel of Wealth, as you can see, land is an imperative part of building your portfolio. You've got to be strategic with your real estate investments; for example, as long as there are universities and polytechnics, college kids will always need accommodation. So why not build real estate around campuses to solve the housing needs of that demographic, and as long as the school churns out students, you'll have a constant supply line to your hostels."

"Man, that's a damn good idea."

"Yeah, that's part of my Wealth Acquisition strategy. I intend to own hostels in every state that has a major university. I already have a few."

"Wehdonesir!" Soma hailed, gesticulating.

"Toks, seriously, I just admire your business acumen. I'm seriously learning that making wealth is intentional, and that having money doesn't make you wealthy."

"Absolutely, wealth is the seed, money is the fruit. That's why when most people lose their money, they can't reproduce it, because all they had was a fruit that eventually got rotten, they never knew how to nurture the seed and ultimately build a system that grows trees and keeps the cycle going."

"True that," concurred Ezzy.

"Glad it's all coming together. Now let's get to the next spoke on the Wheel of Wealth: Debt Elimination."

"I'm very interested in this aspect, I need to be delivered from the spirit of impulsive spending," Soma said, leaning forward.

"That makes two of us. For some reason, I can't walk away from a good deal," Ezzy nodded.

Told smiled as he refilled his glass and took a sip.

"Well, first off, we have to determine if you're dealing with good debt or bad debt."

"I didn't know there were different types of debt," Ezzy remarked.

"Of course there is," Soma replied. "There's good debt, which can be used to fund assets and then there's gbese."

"Isn't all debt gbese?" Ezzy grinned cheekily.

"Well, there are some schools of thought that say that, while others believe debt, like Soma said, falls into two categories, consumer debt aka gbese and investment debt."

"Not sure I know the difference," Ezzy shrugged.

"It's really quite simple. When trying to figure out whether it's good or bad debt, ask the question; is this debt an investment that's going to yield me a profit? If the answer is yes, then it's good debt. If the answer is no, then, it's gbese. For example, taking a loan to build an estate or block of flats, is good debt, because selling the units can yield a profit for you. So good debt makes money for you and bad debt loses money for you."

"But when does good debt become gbese?" Ezzy asked. "Because I've seen people acquire good debt for a good reason at some interesting rates, and after a while, they default for some reason or the other, and all of a sudden, they're in gbese. So isn't it better to just be debt averse from the beginning and avoid stories that touch?"

"That's a great question, bro. The truth is, debt carries a high element of risk. Unfortunately, most people don't weigh the risk involved by asking the question, *what happens if I can't pay back?* Too many folks are lulled into a sense of false security of their own projections, invincibility or invulnerability. Now, I'm gonna say something that sounds a bit counter intuitive; when a bank loans you money, they're hoping you're not going to be able to pay it back."

"Toks, I'm not sure I agree. I'm a banker, remember?"

"I know, dear, but your bank, ultimately, is a business. I know you conduct your risk analysis on every prospect who wants to get a loan, ask them for collateral, which is usually worth more than the loan and given the unfriendly interest rates, somehow or the other, you know there's a fairly good chance he's going to default on the loan."

"Sounds a bit predatory if you ask me," Ezzy said.

"I'll concede the argument, Toks, but I sha know that my bank isn't like that," Soma replied grudgingly.

"On that note, we agree to disagree," Toks said as he sipped his drink.

"So how do we deal with this issue of gbese?" Soma asked.

"First off, I think the major reason people fall into it is because they want more than they can afford and luckily, the items they purchase don't snitch that they were bought on credit; but sadly, their wallets feel the pinch when they have to pay the monthly charges. The second reason is they probably have a subconscious desire to show that they're worth more than they really are, because they think that not having valuable things equates to not being a person of value, but the truth is having valuable things doesn't particularly make you a person of value either--"

"Hmmm. That's deep! *Having valuable things doesn't particularly make you a person of value and not having valuable things does not mean you're not a person of value,"* Soma reiterated as she scribbled furiously into her notepad.

"Yes, Soma, and I believe the final reason people wind up having gbese is because of unforeseen circumstances, emergencies or maybe life gets in the way and they need a helping hand up. So which of the three reasons do you think accounts for your issues with debt?"

"To be honest, Toks, my gbese is definitely self-inflicted. I'd go with numbers one and two."

"I appreciate your honesty."

"Who forming epp? I need to be delivered from myself," she laughed.

"Hey man, what about you? What's your poison?" Toks asked.

"Dude, it's the same as Soma's. Keeping up with the Kardashians or Joneses is pretty tough, but I think there's something missing from your explanation. What about people who borrow, not because they lack, but just because they can't justify spending their own money, so they take from this dude and that dude all without the intention of ever paying back?"

"I hope you're not talking about yourself in this scenario, bro?"

"Nah man, I don't ball like that. I'm just curious. So what do you think?" Ezzy replied.

"Man, those kind of people are just leeches, that's all; blood-sucking leeches. So here's what I want you guys to do. I want you determine how bad your debt is. Imagine your debt profile is between the numbers one to ten, where one is terrible gbese, where the creditors are breaking down your door, causing you to lose sleep and you're dreading bumping into them; while ten is debt free. What's your number?"

"Man, I'd say I'm a solid four, I'm forever paying something off," Ezzy grunted.

"Soma?"

"Same as Ezzy on this one. I just can't seem to resist a good deal and for some weird reason, after I pay one gbese off, I get sucked in to the next one. It's a vicious cycle."

"One you'll just have to stop, because gbese is you sacrificing your future needs for your present desires."

"But first, you'll have to pay off your existing debt. How much do you owe?"

"Man, I'll have to calculate it."

"What about you Soma?"

"Let me take a moment to list them all."

Soma and Ezzy began to itemize their list of creditors while Toks grabbed some peanuts.

"Babe, what's your number?" Soma asked Ezzy, who was staring intently at the ceiling.

"I'm too ashamed to talk about it."

"Don't be. Full disclosure is necessary for debt elimination," Toks said

"Okay, I'll show you mine if you show me yours" Ezzy grinned, a mischievous gleam in his eyes.

"You sure I really shouldn't get James to open up the Guest room?"

"Don't mind him jor. I'll say mine since someone's obviously too chicken. I owe about N483,440 and about N250k of it is the balance on my car loan, and the rest is from the hair, shoes and bags I bought from SimplyLil'."

"Simply who?"

"'SimplyLil, you don't know her jor; she's a stylist and image consultant. The baddest style master in the game. Abeg, she's on Instagram @simplylilspeaksstyle"

"No wonder your style is on point now," Ezzy said.

"So what are you saying, that my style was wack?"

"Thanks Soma," Toks said, defusing a potentially dangerous situation.

"Ezzy, you're up."

"Chai. Where am I gonna start from? Should I include the N500k that went into MMM?"

"No. That's not debt. Those guys have cashed out and are definitely not planning to return any of your money. So that right there, is a loss."

"Okay, I owe N347,780. N150k is for our monthly contribution at the office, N80k is my tab for drinks and meals at The Lounge, then the rest is on that lovely three piece suit I got from OUCH."

"He does make some amazing pieces, doesn't he?"

"Man, his Platinum collection is the truth."

"If you guys have gotten a suitgasm or relived your suit fetish, may I suggest that we proceed?" Soma smirked.

"Eeewww. Suitgasm? That's so gross. How do you come up with these words?" Ezzy grimaced.

"You're not the only wordsmith in the family."

"Okay lovebirds, let's get to another spoke on the Wheel of Wealth, and it's a doozy, it's Insurance."

"Haaaa. Bros, I no gree. This one, we go drag am. I know I've said that Network Marketing and Real Estate are scams, but this one na the king of all scams."

"Toks, I'm with Ezzy on this one. Most insurance companies are scams. You'll actually pay more in premiums than what you'll receive in claims. That's how I'd been paying my premiums religiously and then a month before my car got into an accident with a Danfo, I missed a payment and see me see trouble oh, that's how they said they weren't going to pay for any kind of repair. In fact, the stupid account officer now started speaking English to me, that company policy says...na God save am, I for woz am better slap."

'I hope it's been sorted now?" Toks asked.

"We still dey drag am," she replied.

"Shey you see, bro? Isn't that a scam?" Ezzy asked.

"Yes, I'd admit it. They're a scam, but doesn't that mean that if there are fakes, there must be an original? Listen guys, I know the Nigerian insurance industry has a long way to go and presently leaves a lot to be desired. However, let's not throw the baby out with the bathwater. Why is insurance important?"

"Err...it's not," Ezzy scoffed.

"You've got jokes," Toks smiled. "Insurance is important because it's a safety net for when things go wrong. And since life is guarandamnteed ..."

"Tweetable!" Soma yelled "just because I like that word."

Toks chuckled as he continued.

"Since life is guarandamnteed to be unpredictable as Murphy's law suggests--"

"What's Murphy's law?" asked Ezzy.

"It's an aphorism that says anything that could possibly go wrong, will go wrong," Soma replied.

"Ain't that the truth?" Ezzy concurred.

"If Murphy's law is anything to go by, then it makes sense to take precautions."

"Let me put it this way. While investments help you to get rich, insurance prevents you from dying poor."

"Damn!" Ezzy screamed. "Shit! Dude, you can drop the mic right there."

"As in, Toks, if there was an award for my favorite tweetable, this is it!" Soma clapped as she scribbled into her notebook.

"Investments help you to get rich, insurance prevents you from dying poor."

"Chaaaiiii. Na to get insurance be that."

"At least start with the more important aspects, such as life insurance or your assets. I mean, if JLo can insure her assets, pun intended, for $27 million; Julia Roberts insured her smile for $3 million and Christiano Ronaldo insured his legs for $145 million, doesn't it make sense to insure the goose that lays the golden eggs?"

"But Toks, I agree. But most of these companies are scams."

"Perhaps, but like I've said previously, investigate before you invest. Ask all the hard questions, read the fine print; don't just take their word for it. You need to make sure that if they're willing to take your premiums, they're just as willing to pay out their claims."

"True talk," Ezzy agreed.

"I know that paying insurance might seem like a gamble with the odds ninety-nine to one that nothing would ever happen to you, unless of course in the case of death. You also have to consider that you pretty much forfeit your premiums if nothing ever happens to you, but what about that one in a hundred chance that something does happen? Would you rather bear that kind of risk? Would you rather lose all your investments because you didn't have insurance? It's pretty much being penny wise and pound foolish."

"Hmmm. That's true," Ezzy concurred.

"After spending all my active years building my investments and only to lose it in my passive years because I didn't have insurance? God forbid!" Soma said.

"Nuff said," Toks concurred.

"Now let's get to the final spoke on our Wheel of Wealth, Charitable Giving."

"All the dough wey Charity don gather never do? Toks, leave story, Charity na big babe. Who Charity don epp sef?"

"Abi oh," Soma said, grinning. "Toks, it's true, most people that float NGO's are just fleecing kind-hearted people, and they don't do anything with the donations they get. I read in a newspaper how money, blankets, medicines and food donated to an Internally Displaced Persons camp in the north were diverted by the NGO officials who were now selling these relief materials in the market and keeping the cash."

"I mean, how low can you go?" Ezzy asked.

"Apparently, not low enough." Toks growled. "But truth is, as the scripture says, *the heart of man is desperately wicked*. But that said, we shouldn't throw out the whole basket because of a few bad apples."

"Bros, the whole basket don spoil, na to find good apple be the koko."

"Be that as it may, guys, but there are many trusted platforms that do amazing work, I mean, there's the Irede Foundation that provides prosthetic limbs to children born with congenital defects or child amputees and gives them a new lease on life as well as so many others."

"That's true, I know the founder, Crystal Chigbu, her daughter, Beulah was born with a congenital defect and had to be amputated as an infant. Irede Foundation is legit," Soma said.

"Okay man, I'll bite, but why's Charitable Giving so important?"

"Great question. I don't believe that the purpose of wealth is to get all you can, can all you get and then sit on the can--"

"Dude, how do you come up with all these rhymes?"

"Beats me, man. I'm sure there's a compliment in there somewhere. But as I was saying, the purpose of wealth isn't about getting all you can--"

"Canning all you get," Ezzy interjected.

"And sitting on the can," Soma finished with aplomb.

"You guys are just kids," Toks smiled, shrugging. "Now that we've gotten that out of the way, wealth isn't meant to be stored, it's meant to be shared."

"Tweetable!" Soma cheered as she reached for her notepad and scribbled.

"*Wealth isn't meant to be stored, it's meant to be shared.*"

"Storing money without sharing it is like keeping water in a tank; if there's no inflow or outflow, the water becomes stagnant, begins to stink and ultimately becomes dangerous for consumption. But the most important reason to give charitably, is to show yourself that you're truly money's master and not the other way around."

"That's hard though," Soma said.

"No one said it would be easy, but in reality, giving grows your capacity. Once you've given on a level, I believe it releases you to a new phase of growth. I remember when giving N10k was a big deal to me. I mean when I'd have to give, I'd feel the void it left; for days. I couldn't bring myself to go beyond that level, and to be honest, my income didn't grow beyond what it was either. So I figured that if I couldn't grow my income, I would grow my giving and weirdly enough, I found out that as I gave more, I slowly began to earn more; and besides, as J.K. Rowling once said, *you have a moral responsibility when you've been given far more than you need, to do wise things with it and give intelligently.*"

"Easy for her to say, she's a billionaire," scoffed Ezzy.

"Perhaps, but she wasn't always one. Besides, how many houses does anyone really need? How many bedrooms can you actually sleep in at a time?"

"Bros, that's easy for you to say nah, no be five-bedroom duplex be this?"

"Actually, six, but who's counting. Anyway since you brought it up, I'll use my home as an analogy. Think about wealth like a six-bedroom home. It was created to house, pun intended at least six individuals, one per room and provide comfort and security to them. But because I choose to be selfish, I'll inhabit my home myself, walking around the grounds like the *Ghost of Christmas Past*, sleeping in a different room each night. I have great capacity for more, but since I refuse to be charitable, I can't truly enjoy my wealth."

"Me that I don't like people staying in my house," grumbled Soma.

"So doesn't that defeat the purpose of having a six-bedroom house when you only need two rooms? That's the problem. You want to brag that you live in a six-bedroom duplex, even though all you need is two. Folks are in love with the idea of wealth or success, without realizing there's a responsibility that comes with the power they possess. Listen fellas, I'm reminded of a story about a man who was lost in a desert. After wandering for couple of days, he miraculously stumbled on a well with a water pipe and handle attached. Obviously dying of thirst, he reached for the pipe to slake his thirst, only to realize it was dry. Just as he was about to vent his frustration, he noticed a bottle of water by the edge of the well with a little note attached that said, *if you want water, pour the water in this bottle into the pipe and pump the handle."*

"Pour ke?" Ezzy scoffed. "Omo, na to drink the water finish be dat."

"Perhaps, but the water wouldn't be enough to slake his thirst. What would you do, Soma? Would you drink the water or risk certain death by pouring the bottle's life-giving content back into the pipe?"

"I'm not sure. I'll be honest, I'd probably drink the water too, self-preservation, abi?" Soma said as she covered her face, ashamed.

"I appreciate your honesty, guys and as you can expect, it was a pretty tough decision for this particular individual. So after a few traumatic minutes, he decided to follow the note's instruction. He took the little bottle and emptied its content into the pipe. Exhausted, and with his strength fading fast, he began pumping the handle--"

"Oh my God, I can't bear to know what happened," Soma gasped anxiously.

"He pumped as hard as he could, and for a while, nothing happened. But as he persevered, he began to feel the water pressure rise in the pipe, and before you knew it, life giving water began gushing from the pipe."

"Thank God," said Soma, relieved.

"He not only drank his fill, but was able to wash himself off and even had more than enough to refill his previously empty water bottles and most importantly, the water bottle that made this all possible."

"Oh wow."

"Now refreshed enough to continue his journey, he replaced the full bottle of water and the note, so that other thirsty people could see it and quench their thirst, even as he had."

"Hmm...that's deep." said Ezzy. "Imagine if he had gone with his natural instinct for self-preservation, he would've died."

"But do you know the real hero of the story?" asked Soma.

"I'm sure I have a pretty good idea," Toks said smiling.

"I'm definitely missing something. Wasn't there only one person in this story?" Ezzy scowled, counting his fingers.

"The hero of the story is the person who left the bottle of water there in the first place."

"Exactly!" Toks raised his glass to Soma as he sipped his drink.

"I mean, if he hadn't created a system and left a bottle of water for travelers, who knows how many people would have died of thirst?"

"And that's the main issue isn't it? Every traveler was faced with a choice. Serve yourself and drink what's barely enough for you, or invest in a system that would take care of you and invariably, others. Imagine if one person decided to put himself first, there would never have been enough water to serve anyone else, even though the well had the capacity and content to serve a lot of people. Unfortunately, too many people would rather choose self-preservation and when they gulp all its content, they die, leaving nothing left. And funny enough, the more you give, the more you receive. That's why I insist that the true purpose of wealth is not for storage, but for sharing."

"Amen to that, bro. Tell all these corrupt politicians hiding forex in sewage pits, graves and offices to share the money."

"That's why so many are so poor, because tons of our commonwealth has become personal wealth and isn't being redistributed within the system."

"Abeg, let's leave them. Judgment day is coming," Soma said.

"Can we pass judgment on the judges first? Too bad most of the judiciary's corrupt," Ezzy growled.

"Let's focus on what we can control," Toks continued.

"So here's what I need you to do. I want you to draw a big circle--"

"Like your mothers cooking pot!" Soma and Ezzy sang.

"Jinx!" They said at the same time and high-fived each other.

"You guys are truly something..." Toks grinned as he refilled his glass.

"As I was saying, I'd like you to draw a...sphere. Now once that's done, I'd like you to divide it into eight parts, each of which is going to represent an aspect of the spokes on the Wheel of Wealth. Now, remember that the eight dimensions on the Wheel of Wealth are *Income, Wealth Creation , Savings, Investments, Land and Real Estate, Debt Elimination, Insurance* and *Charitable Giving.* Next step, I'd like you to rate your present level of accomplishment or satisfaction on each level, where 10 is absolutely awesome and 1 is incredibly dismal. Then once that's done, I'd like you to join the dots, so eventually, you'll probably have a circle or some shape within the main circle. Remember to be as honest with yourself as possible, don't put in a best case scenario or be in denial, because as you know, garbage in is garbage out. This assessment can't be effective if it's doctored."

Soma and Ezzy began working as Toks flipped channels on the TV.

"How's it coming fellas? How round is your circle?"

"I'm not sure I can call this thing a circle oh," Ezzy groaned.

"Me neither. This diagram looks like it should be in a Further Mathematics textbook," Soma concurred.

"Let me see. Let's start from you, bro. What were your scores for each of the dimensions?"

"This is pretty embarrassing, but I'm gonna take it like a man, so here goes: *Income 5, Wealth creation 3 , Savings 2, Investments 1, Land and real estate 0, Debt elimination 2, Insurance 0* and *Charitable Giving 0."*

"You're right, definitely embarrassing," Toks grinned.

"Haaa.That means you can't see my own oh, Toks. If you're making fun of Ezzy, you'll flip out with mine," Soma said, trying to hide her notebook.

"No, I'm just kidding. Please Soma, I promise I won't laugh."

"Okay, here goes. *Income 4, Wealth creation 2 , Savings 1, Investments 1, Land and real estate 1, Debt elimination 4, Insurance 3* and *Charitable Giving 2."*

"Err, sorry babe. Did you say you scored one in Land and Real Estate? Is there something you're not telling me?" Ezzy frowned.

"Relax honey, you forgot that you gave me some money to keep for you when you got a bonus at the office a few years ago."

"Hmm…I kind of remember," Ezzy said, scratching his head.

"You got a bonus and you were planning to add some money to buy a car, but gave it to me for safe keeping?"

"Chai, I remember now. See this babe, how come I forgot it with you after all this time?"

"I knew that if I didn't bring up the subject of the car with you, you'd eventually forget it, so I used it to buy a plot of land from LandWey and also bought one from Nedcom Oaks; those real estate guys for us."

"Good thinking," Toks said.

"But you should have told me nah. That's how some husbands find out that their wives have bought real estate and built houses without their knowledge. I mean, I heard a story about a guy who was trying to surprise his wife, so they could move into a bigger apartment, he called an agent who scheduled a meeting with the owner, who just happened to be his wife. Na so gbege come bust and marriage come scatter."

"You're right. I'm sorry," Soma apologized.

"Okay, now that paradise is restored, Soma, let me take a look at your wheel again."

"Ohhh and I hoped you'd forgotten."

"Not a chance. What did you say your numbers were again?"

"*Income 4, Wealth creation 2 , Savings 1, Investments 1, Land and real estate 1, Debt elimination 4, Insurance 3* and *Charitable Giving 2.*"

"Okay, your numbers are pretty similar to Ezzy. So you both don't have a wheel as much as you do a funny looking shape."

"So how do we get our wheels spinning as they should?" Ezzy asked.

"Maybe you should join the Hallelujah Challenge," Toks laughed, "Let Olowogbogboro do it suddenly."

"Hallelujah what? Olowo wetin?" Ezzy asked confused.

"See this guy oh. Abi you've been sleeping on a bicycle? Don't go and say it outside!" Soma scoffed.

"What nah? Am I missing something?" Ezzy asked.

"Before nko? So, for the last two weeks that I've been waking up at midnight to pray, what did you think I was doing?"

"Err...disturbing the peace and my sleep? I always wondered why you were watching Instagram and praying at the same time."

"The Bible says watch and pray, didn't it?" Soma answered.

"Nice clap back, Soma, very well played," Toks clapped. "You've gotta hand it to your wife, bro, she gives as good as she gets."

"So that you don't disgrace me and say it outside, allow me to school you. The Hallelujah Challengeis a prayer meeting that Nathaniel Bassey--"

"Nathaniel who?"

"I don't believe this," Soma groaned as she continued, "You know that track you always ask me to put on repeat in the car?"

"*30 billion for the account oh*...that one?" Ezzy said as he began to dance. "I no know say the guy na Pastor."

"Chineke biko kwa," Soma exclaimed as Toks burst into laughter.

"No jor. Not that track. The other one. The gospel one."

"Oh okay...that guy? That's him? He's a correct guy."

"Thank you, Jesus. Yes, that guy. Nathaniel Bassey started a praise and worship session, called the Hallelujah Challenge that he livestreams at midnight for an hour on Instagram and Facebook. Over one hundred thousand people around the world join in for an hour of praise and worship to God. He started it a couple years ago and does it in seasons now, each time for a number of days."

"Ah ah. Is that how we are? So why haven't you involved me? You don't think I want to praise God abi?" Ezzy asked.

"Mttsscheeww," Soma hissed. "How convenient. Now that this one is almost finished is when you want to participate. When I was trying to involve you since, did you agree? Abeg, park at a corner."

"Oya oya, remind me tonight. I'll join in and who knows, maybe our finances will take a turn for the better."

"Hallelujah to that, man. From your mouth to God's ear. But while you give it to God, remember that it's important to give God something to work with." Toks said.

"True. So what happens next with the wheel?"

"Simple. Your goal over the next couple of months is to make the right financial decisions that will increase each of those dimensions. That way, as each dimension grows, the rounder your circle gets. And since it's a wheel of wealth, realize that wealth is a wheel that spins as fast as you push."

"Tweetable!" Soma said as she reached for her notepad.

"Wealth is a wheel that spins as fast as you push."

"So the sooner you get pushing on each of these dimensions, the faster your wealth grows," Toks said.

"Eventually, as you build systems around your wealth, your wheel begins to spin faster. The key is to build a system that's 100% independent of you."

"And that's the challenge. We're up to it," Soma said, taking her husband's hands in hers.

"I was hoping you'd say that," Toks smiled, walking into his study.

"Err...why do I feel like we just walked into a trap?" Soma asked.

"Because we did," Ezzy grinned.

Toks returned, armed with a couple of printed sheets of paper.

"Okay fellas, you're gonna be taking part in my 4-by-30 Total Money Workout Challenge!"

"I don't like the sound of that," Ezzy groaned.

"I thought you guys said you were up to it?" Toks grinned as he handed over the sheets of paper.

"Yes we are," Soma said, staring at her husband intently and pinching him.

"Yeeee! I mean Ouchhhh! Yeah, yeah, we are."

"Good to know we're on the same page," Toks smiled. "Alright, let's get to it."

"So, for the next seven days, I'd like you to work on a few exercises, nothing over the top."

"We can do that," Soma grinned nervously, "Fire away."

"Great. So for Day One, I'd like you to calculate your net worth.

"How do we do that?" Ezzy asked

"It's our total assets minus our total liabilities," Soma replied.

"Remind me to deal with this in detail afterwards," Toks said.

"Okay, cool."

"For Day Two, I'd like you to itemize what I call your spending triggers. By that, I mean, what people, event, emotions or things put you in the mood to spend money?"

"I'm looking at her." Ezzy laughed as Soma reached for him, missed and then threw a pillow at him.

"If I catch you…" Soma chuckled.

"Toks, abi na lie?" Ezzy asked.

"I'd rather not be a victim of a double homicide, so I'll pass on the question," Toks demurred.

"For real, bro, Soma is a spending trigger because according to your definition, it's people, event, emotions or things put you in the mood to spend money. My wife is a person that when you don't give her money, it becomes an event, she throws around her emotions and she'll end up doing unpleasant things to you."

"Chai, see my life, Ezzy has finished me," Soma blushed. "Shey we're going home in the same car, we shall see."

"Toks, is the offer to use your Guest room still open?" Ezzy asked.

Toks smiled, "Not anymore."

"Abeg, Toks, don't mind your friend, can you talk about these spending triggers in detail?"

"Sure thing. Everyone has something that causes them to spend money they didn't plan for. For example, some people tend to be more generous with themselves or with others when they get a raise or sudden inflow of cash. This particular spending trigger is usually known as lifestyle inflation."

"Hmmm...sounds like I'm guilty of this one," Soma said, scribbling.

"So when your paycheck gets bigger, ideally, so should your ability to pay off your gbese or increase your financial goals. But unfortunately, that's when we tend to splurge on some unnecessary gizmo or gadget."

"I won't lie, all I've been thinking about since I saw the Ad, is getting an iPhone 11"

"Exactly! So a little extra cash gathered from extra income or just from being prudent creates a spending trigger that causes you to reach for your wallet and splurge."

"So how do you resist the temptation?"

"Before pulling out your wallet, ask yourself four questions. One: What is the feeling that I will experience after I've made this purchase?"

"I'll feel great cause if I have the iPhone 11, I'll be the biggest, baddest babe on the block."

"Fantastic! So this leads to my second question, Soma. How long is that feeling going to last?"

"Only until someone else I know gets it, which might be a few hours to a few days."

"So here's my third question. Now that all your friends have the iPhone 11, does your purchase really seem worth it?"

"No jor. I'll just spend over $1,000 to make my friends jealous for a few days until they now vex and launch theirs."

"Sounds like it'll give you short term returns on your long term investment. So this leads to my final question, so this feeling of jealousy you'd like to evoke in your friends, is there a free or less expensive way to achieve it?"

"Well, I guess it's to become financially fit and free. Not just by having the trappings of success like the iPhone X, which maybe in my former life, I would have taken a loan to buy and paid it off over a year, and none except me would be the wiser, even though that would've been a foolish decision. So I guess, if I can get my act together and build a high quality life, with no gbese or baggage, I'll become the reference point and perhaps the envy of all my friends."

"Nuff said."

"So are there any other spending triggers?" Ezzy asked.

"You bet. For some, loneliness, sadness or anger are triggers. You get in a mood, and just decide to window shop or surf the Internet, and before you know it, you're on a 'retail therapy' binge. For others, it's the feeling of 'I deserve it'."

"That's me right there. I mean, I hustle hard, I bust my ass at work. It's only fair that I treat myself to some nice things. I mean, a watch here, a gadget there ain't gonna hurt," Soma said.

"Perhaps, but the truth is, it all piles up and before you know it, you've got a closet stacked with things you really didn't need."

"But Toks, what if it's on sale and the deal's too good to resist?" Soma asked.

"That's one of the strongest and most powerful spending triggers. Everyone wants a good deal. So when you see promotions like *Buy One, Get One Free* or a *50% Discount, it* makes you feel like you're getting a good deal, but the truth is, it's only a deal if you were planning to buy it in the first place, if not, you're buying for the thrill of it."

"Yeah, shopping for thrills. Guilty as charged," Soma said.

"So the next time you feel the urge to scratch that spending itch, what are the questions you're meant to ask yourself?"

"What is the feeling that I will experience after I've made this purchase?" Soma said, checking her notes.

"Yup, what else?"

"How long is that feeling going to last?"

"Only as long as it takes to finish my Aleda Dolce ice cream." Toks replied with a chuckle.

"Aleda who?"

"Oh, you haven't heard? They're the coolest ice cream parlor in PH, they make some incredible rolled ice cream and gelato, and so whenever I have to go see Momsy, I always have to buy for her before I get home. You should check them out on Instagram @aleda_dolce "

"Oshey gelato! DJ Cuppy omo Otedola!" Ezzy said, hailing his wife.

"Abeg shifti" Soma laughed, waving her hand at her husband. "Toks please, what's the third question?" she asked.

"Is your purchase really worth it?"

"And the final one?"

"I wrote it this way. Is there a free or less expensive way to achieve the feeling that the purchase provides?"

"Very well said, Soma. Is there a free or less expensive way to achieve the feeling that the purchase provides? So that's what I'd like you to handle for Day Two."

"Sounds like a plan. So what about Day Three?"

"I thought you would never ask. I'd like you to have a Clean House."

"Err…not sure how long it's been since you've been at our crib and what you remember from your last visit, but I'm pretty sure we've got a clean house." Ezzy said, scratching his head.

"That's not what he means jare. He's talking about looking through our stuff to find things we don't need and put them on sale."

"That's definitely a good idea, if we sell those clothes you keep dreaming of fitting into, we'd be rich."

"If I slap you…" Soma launched a pillow at her husband.

"I guess that's why they call it a throw pillow," Toks said, sipping his drink.

"As I was saying to you lovebirds, if you look through your closet, and perhaps around the house, you'll discover you've picked up a few things that you really don't need, and could sell at a bargain."

"Yeah, we could put some things on OLX and…"

"Sell it!" they chorused in unison.

"Jinx!" they said at the same time, again.

"Now that you both double-jinxed, how about you both keep quiet until I say your names; that way, I can get a few words in?"

Soma and Ezzy smiled and nodded while Toks continued.

"So once you've sold out, remember to keep the money in a savings account that you're not touching for a period of time. We good so far?"

Soma and Ezzy nodded in agreement.

"Now for Day Four, you're gonna Keep The Change."

Ezzy raised a hand, a mischievous smile on his face.

"I'm not so sure I want you to speak," Toks said, sipping his drink.

Soma raised a hand.

“Yes, Soma. Drats, just said your name.”

“Yippee! Now we can have some peace and quiet while Ez…err...I mean this guy sits pretty until we say his name.”

“Agreed. So where were we?”

“You said something about keeping the change.”

Ezzy raised a hand again.

“There goes our peace and quiet, I know I'm going to regret this.”

“Oooooh, Toks, don't release Ezzy nah, that's how he won't let us rest…oops!”

Ezzy bolted out of his seat, dancing around the room in excitement. “You can't keep a good man down! Anybody wey say my gari no go don, their water no go boil!”

“Abeg, park at a corner,” Soma scoffed.

“I'm with Soma on this one. Let's keep it moving. I've lost my train of thought. Where were we?”

“Keep the change, bae! I've been itching to say that since,” Ezzy yelled.

“Mttsscchheewwww, you're not serious. Please Toks, don't mind your friend, continue.”

“I know these things may seem rudimentary, mundane, even; but like I've said before, small keys open big doors and besides, if you don't find out where you're leaking from, you'll be filling a bucket with many teeny, tiny holes.”

“Word!”

Toks continued. “So here's what I'd like you to do with the Keep The Change challenge. I assume you leave home with a specific amount of money?”

“Err…”

Ezzy and Soma looked at each other nervously.

"Okay, scratch that, I assume you leave home with an ATM card and spend what you need from there, right?"

"That's more like it," Ezzy grinned.

"Not anymore. From now on and for the next month, you're going to be restricted to a daily spending limit."

"So we don't spend more from our ATM cards?"

"I'd rather you withdraw the amount in cash and not touch your ATM card after that."

"See set up!"

"That's the whole idea. So you withdraw a specific amount of money daily and whatever ends up not being spent is put into an envelope."

"But what if the money I withdraw isn't enough?" Soma asked.

"Then, you either make sure it is or you decide what's really important and cut down on what's not."

"This is so going to be hard," Soma said.

"Nothing good comes easy, else we'd all have private jets, have six packs and not have to work a single day in our lives," Toks replied.

"True that. So what happens next?" Ezzy asked.

"After thirty days, I'd like you to take out the envelope and count how much you saved, simply by keeping the change."

"Might not be a lot of money though," Ezzy mumbled.

"Perhaps, but let's do a bit of math. Imagine you saved five hundred bucks each day that was untouched for thirty days? How much would that be?"

"15k."

"Now imagine if you saved 15k for a year. How much would that be?"

"180k. That's not small money oh," Ezzy concurred.

"And that's just from keeping the change. Imagine if you saved N1,000 a day? That's literally, double what you got at N500. Now imagine that every month, you decided to save or invest in something that could possibly give you perhaps 10% interest?"

"That's some serious money saved."

"Yeah and when in doubt, you can leave it in a fixed deposit account or invest in T. Bills."

"Invest in TBillz? Is his entertainment company looking for investors? Didn't he just sign Tacha? The guy don blow nah" Ezzy said.

"Jesus, Mary and Joseph," Toks said, shaking his head. "I think I need a stronger drink."

"Ezekiel ohhh! This man won't disgrace me outside. Toks meant Treasury Bills not TBillz, Tiwa Savage's husband." Soma screamed, pulling her husband's ear.

"Ouuucchhh! Why didn't you just say so nah? You people will be confusing somebody."

"Now you know how I feel," Toks said, pouring another drink.

"Remember guys, you can't earn your way into a fortune, you've gotta deliberately make money your slave."

"Unfortunately many of us are tied up as slaves to money," Soma said.

"Speaking of being tied up, let's talk about your network."

TOTAL MONEY WORKOUT

1. Here's your Wheel of Wealth. Score each section according to how satisfied you are with it at the moment on a scale of 0 (low) – to 10 (high). Mark each score on the appropriate spoke of your wheel. Now join up the marks around the circle. How does your wheel of wealth look? Is it balanced? Where you scored the lowest are the areas that need the greatest amount of work.

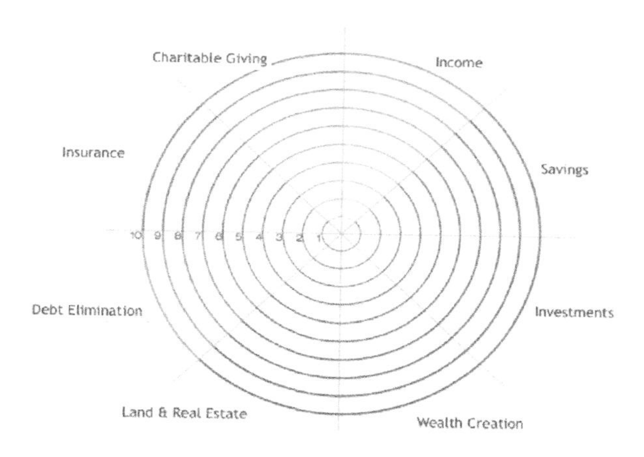

2. Next it's time to consider your ideal level in each area of your wheel. A balanced wheel does not mean getting 10 in each financial area: some areas need more attention and focus than others at any time. And inevitably you will need to make choices and compromises, as your time and energy are not in unlimited supply! So the question is, what would the ideal level of attention be for you in each financial area? Plot the "ideal" scores around your this wheel too.

3. Once you have identified the areas that need attention, it's time to plan the actions needed to work on regaining balance. Starting with the neglected areas, what things do you need to start doing to regain balance? Make a commitment to these actions by writing them down.

4. What past experiences are determining your present circumstances? Think them over and write them down.

5. What experiences have you associated with failure?

6. Who can you associate business success with? Who do you know that has succeeded in business?
7. How much debt do you have? Break them down and list them. Now, focus on either paying off the largest debt first (partly or in full) and then work your way down.
8. It's time for your 4-by-30 Total Money Workout Challenge

- Day 1: Calculate your net worth

ASSETS	LIABILITIES

- Day 2: What are your spending triggers? What people, event, emotions or things put you in the mood to spend money?
- Day 3: It's time to Clean House. Look through your stuff to find things you don't need and put them on sale
- Day 4: Keep the Change: restrict yourself to a specific amount of money withdrawn in cash from your ATM. Whatever doesn't get spent gets put into an envelope. Continue this for 30 days.
- Day 30: Take all money made from the Clean House & Keep the Change challenge and put it in a Fixed Deposit account

CHAPTER 11

ARE YOUR NETS WORKING?

Secret 11: Your nets' work first determines your network, which eventually determines your net worth.

The work you do determines the people you know, but the people who know you determine the money you make.

"Speaking of being tied up, let's talk about your network," Toks continued.

"I'm sure my signal is poor around here, I can't even browse; this my network won't let me be great," Ezzy said, looking at his phone.

"That's a pretty good way to look at it," Toks said, smiling.

"Oh, do you use GNettoo? I'm sure the owner doesn't even use it sef."

"That's not what I mean, bro, but no, I don't use it."

"I was getting a little confused myself, wondering what it had to do with your network," Soma interjected.

"I understand, but I'm using what Ezzy said as a metaphor. What was that thing you said, bro?"

"That the owner doesn't use his network, abi?"

"No, before that, you said *my signal is poor, my network won't let me be great.*"

"Yeah, true that, they'll give you plenty data so cheap that you can't even afford to browse, all these money-taking networks that keep changing their names, abeg, I'll score all these mobile telcos an F9."

"You and me both," Soma concurred.

"Let's put it this way. Wealth, or let's call it success, emits a frequency that only others in that coverage area connect with and are attracted to. So if your success signal is poor, you won't connect to that network of successful people. That's why you've heard the saying that your network determines your net worth." Toks said.

"Yeah, it's a pretty common cliché, but it doesn't tell you how to network with the people that have the network, cause sometimes when I attend all these events that have all these big women in business there, I'm either too intimidated to say hi, or when I do, they'll be carrying face and shoulder for somebody and talking to their cliques. Awon Oloriburuku, abeg, I cannot come and go and kill myself," Soma said.

"That's because you don't know the value of your net."

"I'm sorry, Toks, I don't follow."

"Let me explain it this way. Your nets' work determines your network, which eventually determines your net worth."

"Sounds like a heck of a lotta nets to me," Ezzy grinned.

"I'll explain. The problem most people have with networking is that they already come disadvantaged. They network expecting to be recipients or beneficiaries, instead of realizing that networking is first an introduction of value."

"Tweetable!" Soma said as she scribbled on her trusty notepad

"Networking is an introduction of value."

"But if you don't know the value of your net, how would you be able to communicate it?"

"True that," Ezzy said.

"Most people approach networking from the perspective of *what's in it for me?* Instead of asking, *what's in me for it?What value do I bring to the table?*" Toks replied

"And that value is in first understanding the value of my nets, yeah?" Soma asked.

"Absolutely."

"So how do I do that?" Soma asked reaching for a handful of peanuts.

"If you remember, I said your nets' work determines your network, which eventually determines your net worth. So let's first determine how your net works. Your net is your vehicle for exchange, either being your job or your business and how you perceive the value it brings."

"But what if you don't consider what you do valuable?" Ezzy asked.

"Then you've already placed a ceiling on your network, because no one is attracted to trash, well, except maybe dumpster divers."

"Preach," Soma said.

"Listen guys, you need to understand that business is the intersection where your passion and profit meet."

"Don't say it," Ezzy said, his hand over Soma's mouth.

"Tweetable,"he said, laughing as Soma thumped him with a throw pillow.

"Oya sorry, I know you want to write it." He handed her the notebook.

"Business is the intersection where your passion and profit meet" Soma wrote and then asked "but what happens if your passion isn't making profit?"

"Then you have a hobby," Toks replied.

"Damn!" Ezzy said, "that's just cold."

"Yeah, but the truth will definitely warm you up, so, let me do you one better. If your business isn't involving your passion, you've got a job."

"Oh deep gan," Soma hailed.

"Sounds like me right now," said Ezzy, "the only snag is that I ain't got a business yet, but I'm engaged to a job that I hate."

"You better call off the engagement before you walk down the aisle."

"Too late, bruv, I've signed on the dotted line. I need a good divorce lawyer to break us up without having to pay alimony for the rest of my life."

"I definitely have a job too," Soma chimed in. "Going to work is such a drag these days."

"But guys, don't you see that's the problem? You already feel your net's broken or downright worthless. Think about it this way, when last did you brag to anyone about your job?"

"Err, when I first got it," Soma laughed.

"Can't remember when last I did, man," Ezzy said ruefully. "All I seem to do now is nag and bitch about it."

"So when you nag about a job you hate, would you be interested in communicating its value to anyone?"

"Guess not." Soma shrugged.

"That action automatically limits your network, because you're not proud of it and since you're not, no one is gonna want to associate with it either."

"True that. But Toks, let me hit you from another perspective, you know as an Ad executive, I get to schmooze with some of these heavy hitters at some events."

"Yeah?"

"So my ish isn't about finding it difficult to network, that comes easy; but I feel so sleazy asking for business. Like that's what I wanted all along."

"Yeah, like how you asked me to go out with you, but all you really wanted was to get some," Soma said, laughing.

"And I did, didn't I?" Ezzy smiled coyly.

"Eventually, but not on the first couple of dates jare."

"Huh? I could've sworn we went to my place after we made out in the car at Afolabi's gig--" Ezzy ducked as a a throw pillow narrowly missed his head.

"That would've made some best man speech if I was at your wedding," Toks laughed.

"But here's the point, guys. You need to realize that what you do is an introduction of value and as long as you can communicate that value in a way that's valuable to them--"

"That's deep; *as long as you communicate the value in a way that's valuable to them.*" Soma said, scribbling in her notepad.

"Absolutely, the value you provide must be valuable to the customer, not just to you. Too many people are interested in talking about the value they provide, instead of what it does for the client. I mean, it's in answering that age old question--"

"What would Jesus do?" Ezzy interrupted.

"You've got jokes, bro. It's answering the question, *what's in it for me?* The key to selling value without being salesy is in showing the client how your value increases their value."

"Hmm...that's deep and tweetable." Soma said, scribbling in her notepad. *"Show the client how your value increases their value."*

"Yes Soma, but in order to do this, you're gonna have to realize that people do business with people they know, like and trust."

"Know, Like and Trust – KLT. It's a core feature of subliminal messaging that we use in Advertising. I feel you, Toks. I like to think these Ad execs know me,*like* me even, but I think I'm pretty low on trust's Richter scale."

"That's definitely gotta change, bro, you must become a trusted authority in your field."

"But Toks, how do you do that?" Soma asked.

"It's all about building expertise. Over the last couple of years on your job, by virtue of routine, you've developed some sort of, let me say, muscle memory by working your job; certain things are on autopilot for you, you do them without thinking. But the problem many people have is in not knowing how to project their expertise."

"Amen to that. That's me right there," Soma said. "I know quite a lot, but I'm afraid to share what I know, because one part of me wonders, *what would people think?*, or *what gave me the right to say I'm an authority in anything?*, *what's my track record?*, or the one that kills me, *won't people think I'm arrogant?*"

"And what if they do? Listen Soma, you can't live under the weight of people's unrealistic and unfair expectations of you."

"I know, Toks, but you know how we are in this society, people expect you to be humble, next thing, someone would now say I'm carrying shoulder or that I'm proud."

"And so, you're willing to dim your shine because people can't stand your light?"

"I see what you did there bro, nice!" Ezzy grinned, raising a glass.

"Listen Soma, there's a significant difference between false humility, or as I prefer to call it, *humbility.* I know, I know, it's bad English, but stay with me. There's a difference between *Humbility*, Humility and Arrogance."

"Okay, I'm listening."

"Yeah, me too," Ezzy said, pulling his seat closer.

"Okay, let's get into this. *Humbility* is false humility. That's what we do when for example, someone says, *Great job, Soma* and then you reply with something like, *Na God.*"

Soma burst out laughing.

"I say it all the time, but I say *Baba God noni.*"

"And why do you say it?"

"Well, I don't want anyone to feel I'm being proud by saying something else."

"Something else like what? What would you have really liked to say?"

"Well, I'd really have liked to say, *I know.*"

"Wooohoooo! That's my girl!" Ezzy screamed, clapping. "Come and collect some accolades."

"My guy, keep your accolades, I want assurance now."

"Small Davido no go put grown ass man for trouble."

"Amen oh!" Toks agreed, smiling. "So here's the ish, Soma puts up a front of humility because she doesn't want to come off as smug or proud, but what she doesn't know is that the more she does that, the more that behavior is reinforced in her subconscious mind and soon, it becomes her default behavior. So when an opportunity comes for her to pitch or sell herself, she can't, because she's subconsciously learned this reinforced behavior. You become what you behave."

"That's true," Soma agreed. "I've been living in false humility so long, I barely recognize myself."

"I barely recognize you sometimes with all the makeup you got going on," Ezzy grinned.

“Low blow,” Toks said, backing away as Soma threw a pillow, missed and picked up her shoe.

“Weh done!” Soma said, clapping. “Shey we're going home together, abi? You'll see na.”

“Going home with who? Toks, abeg shey that Guest suite still dey?”

“It's occupied. Y'all better leave me out of this.”

“You gonna leave a brotha hanging, man? Whatever happened to the Bro Code?”

“It's been hacked. Oya, let's continue. Soma, drop the shoe, I'm sure there are more subtle ways to get back at Ezzy.”

“You'll never see me coming.” Soma snapped her fingers at Ezzy who just rolled his eyes.

“Weh done, Thanos. Be snapping finger there,” Ezzy said, getting the last word as Soma reached out for him again.

“Come, guy, no dey use me as bulletproof vest. I'm taking all the hits,” Toks protested, pushing Ezzy into the line of Soma's barrage of well-aimed slaps.

“Okay, now that's out of the way,” Toks said, smiling. Ezzy lay sprawled in pain on the sofa while Soma sat on him, grinning from ear to ear.

“Let's get back to it. We were talking about *humbility* or false humility. My definition of that is making yourself small so that others feel big.”

“Tweetable!” Ezzy yelled from his vanquished position. Soma bounced on him as she wrote in her trusty notepad “*Humbility is making yourself small so that others feel big.*”

“But that's so true, Toks. You keep making yourself small, so that others have an inflated sense of importance. It's all about worrying about what others think about you. No more oh, abeg, who humbility epp?”

“I couldn't have said it better myself,” Toks said.

"So how would you define real humility?" Ezzy asked, moving Soma aside to get off the couch

"That's easy," Toks answered. "It's recognizing you're big, but you're not trying to make anyone feel small."

"Hmmm. That's deep right there," Ezzy said mulling it over.

"Tweetable!" Soma said, scribbling.

"I expected that," Toks said, grinning.

"I subconsciously wonder how many tweetables I can get from you in a day," Soma said, smiling.

"But bro, that's epic right there; what you said about humility…recognizing you're big, but not trying to make anyone feel small."

"Absolutely. You don't need to dumb yourself down to make yourself acceptable. Real humility is about owning your greatness and not apologizing for it simply because you want to fit in with folks who are intimidated by it."

"True that," Ezzy concurred.

"You're a football buff, let me ask you something. Would you say Cristiano Ronaldo is arrogant or humble?"

"The guy is effingarrogant! I mean, when he scores and then does his trademark pose; or when he struts and takes a deep breath before he takes his free kick; what's he feeling like? Abegiii, CR7 is one arrogant mofo."

"I thought you'd say that," Toks said. "What about you Soma? What do you think about Ronaldo?"

"To be honest, before this conversation, I'd have agreed with Ezzy, but since you explained humility as recognizing that you're a big deal and not trying to make others feel small, or like you said – sorry, let me read from my notes…okay, I found it. You said, *real humility is about owning your greatness and not apologizing for it, simply because you want to fit in with folks who are intimidated by it.* Ronaldo recognizes he's a big deal, and he definitely owns it, but it's those of us who are insecure that feel intimidated because somewhere on the inside of us, we wish we could be that confident and secure, so we begrudge him and others who live life on their own terms."

"I couldn't have said it better myself," Toks said.

"So how would you describe arrogance, bro?" Ezzy asked.

"Uncle, I," Soma said, raising her hand like a little child.

"Okay Soma, you've got the floor. How would you define arrogance?" Toks asked.

"Well, we defined Humbility as making yourself small so that others feel big."

"Yeah," Toks agreed.

"Then you said that Humility is recognizing you're big, but you're not trying to make anyone feel small."

"Yeah, absolutely."

"Therefore, it stands to reason that arrogance would be recognizing you're big and deliberately going out of your way to make others feel small."

"Ten points for Soma," Toks said.

"This my babe know book sha," Ezzy said, clapping.

"So now that you understand these definitions, you can live true to yourself, knowing you're not trying to dumb down who you are for people who are sadly, too dumb to know the difference."

"Savage, but I like it," Soma said, grinning.

"That's the ugly truth," Ezzy said.

"Yup, but ugly never looked this good," Toks winked.

"Aaaaaarrggggghhh!Bad guy! Ugly never looked this good," Ezzy repeated, clapping.

"As in," Soma said, "see clap back!"

"Thank you, you're far too kind," Toks said, raising his glass to make a toast.

"So now that we've gotten that out of the way, let's tie this all to your net worth. There's a school of thought that says it's who you know that determines your net worth--"

"Omo, it's true oh. These streets ain't loyal. If you ain't got no friends in high places, you'll remain low in life," Ezzy said.

"I can't believe I'm about to say this and I know I'm going to regret this--" Soma muttered.

"Regret what?" Ezzy asked.

"Tweetable," Soma said, scribbling Ezzy's unusually profound words into her notepad.

"Aaarrgghhh! I told y'all I'm the real deal! This is my *adeniny.* A prophet don't gat no respect in his own home. Call me Alcatraz, cause I've got these bars on lockdown," Ezzy said, pumping his fist in the air and dancing around the room.

"I'm not going to hear the last of this," Soma said, shaking her head.

"This is only the beginning," Toks concurred. "Oya guy, calm down, let's wrap this up."

Ezzy kept on dancing as Toks continued.

"As I was saying before Ezzy dropped his words of wisdom--"

"You won't let us hear word now, Mr. Words of Wisdom," Soma said, dragging her husband to his seat.

"Toks, please continue, your friend is determined to milk this moment for all its worth."

“If I know Ezzy, he'll milk it, make yoghurt from it and churn it into cheese. Anyway, as I was saying, there's a school of thought that says it's who you know that determines your net worth--”

“Yeah, it's a pretty packed school,” Ezzy said.

“Well, you need to drop out because I disagree. It's not who you know that determines your net worth; it's actually who knows you.”

“Run that by me again, bro.”

“It's not who you know that determines your net worth, it's actually who knows you that determines your net worth. Think it over this way, knowing Aliko isn't going to do you much good.”

“*Eligweeelee*! Wait, did you just call Dangote by his first name? Dude don't tell me you're on a first name basis with Dangote? I don die. Guy, you don blow!” Ezzy exclaimed, hands on his head.

“Let's focus on the matter at hand,” Toks said, dismissing his friend's statement.

“Knowing…Aliko isn't going to do you much good if he doesn't know why he needs you.”

“That's true,” Soma agreed “I mean, as a banker, I get to meet with many HNI's or High Networth Individuals, who usually give me their business cards. I have a stack of cards with their names on them, but fear no gree make I call them. I have to introduce myself each time I call them, and when it draws a blank as it often does, I have to mention my bank. Truth be told, I can't do anything for them, they have my M.D. on speed dial.”

“My point exactly! It's all about what you can do for them; which ultimately determines what they can do for you.”

“So if you can't do nothing for them, they can't do squat for you.”

“Diddlysquat. So what problem should they have that's urgent and important for your name to be the solution?”

"Can't think of anything at the moment. That sucks." Soma said.

"Give it time, remember, this is a process. Focus on asking yourself the right questions, the answers will come."

"That's simple, but yet so profound. That's definitely a tweetable," Soma said, writing it down.

"Focus on asking yourself the right questions, the answers will come."

"Speaking of questions. Do you guys know your net worth?" Toks asked

"Man, I have no idea. I'm always intrigued when they say Bill Gates is worth $80 billion. I mean, just lai dat? How do they even calculate it sef?"

"Well, I know we touched on it in one of my banking courses, but to be honest, I'm not exactly sure how it works and why I should care," Soma said.

"Well, it helps in giving you some sort of financial valuation. In a nutshell, your net worth is really everything you own of significance; in this case, your assets minus what you owe in debts, which are your liabilities. So your net worth measures your financial health because it says what you would have left if you sold all of your assets to pay all of your debts. Every financial move you make should be aimed at increasing your net worth. This means either increasing assets, or decreasing liabilities."

"But like Soma said, why should I care?"

"First off, it gives you a snapshot of your current financial position and most importantly, helps you measure your progress as you reach for your financial goals."

"Wawu! Oya nah, let's go there. I'm sure my net worth is off the charts."

"Let's find out," Toks said, smiling.

"So what do we do first?" Soma asked.

"Well, let's start by listing all your assets. You can list them on the left side of your column. Let's start from the money in your savings or current account."

"Check," Ezzy said, checking his phone for his account balance.

"Next up is any money in your fixed deposit account."

"Err…zero," Ezzy said.

"N300k and some change," Soma said.

"This babe, are you for real?" Ezzy said.

"You didn't ask, so I didn't tell," Soma smiled. "Toks, please continue."

"Any T.Bills?" Toks asked.

"No, shey they said he was vexing that Tiwa's dating WizKid," Ezzy grinned.

"That's just savage," Soma smiled. "But walahi, that their *Fever* video no be small."

"See how Tiwa just dey climb WizKid anyhow like say he be ladder."

"Shey he's a StarBoy, he'll help her reach the stars."

"She's a super star na. Make them hold T.Billz oh, na play dem dey play oh."

"Let's move on guys," Toks broke up the fun, chuckling, "they're on another planet."

"Yes oh, Cloud 9," Soma said as they all laughed. "See as everywhere stew."

"Stew? I'm not sure I follow."

"Haa bro, where've you been? You no know stew? You no see as Soma just stew everywhere?"

"Like tinned tomatoes?" Toks asked, shaking his head.

"Tinned tomatoes ke? Me that I'm farm fresh tomatoes." Soma grinned.

"I'm not going to pretend I know what you're both on about," Toks said.

"Stew is just a street slang, for someone hot and fresh, usually women, who look amazing."

"Ah, got it!" Toks grinned. "Oya, moving on, any pensions or retirement funds stashed away."

"Check," the couple said simultaneously.

"Any stock or shares?"

"Check."

"Man, the stock I bought isn't even worth N200k, and the last stock market crash didn't even help."

"Don't worry bro, it happened to us all."

"Any land or real estate?"

"Well, you already told us land isn't an asset if it's not earning for you."

"And I stand by that, but for the purpose of this exercise, let's leave it as an asset. You're however going to place the value at cost price."

"Ope oh! I was just about to cry," Soma said, heaving a sigh of relief.

"You can also include any other assets you might think of. Now once that's done, let's calculate our liabilities."

"Gbese re oooo." Soma exclaimed.

"Any outstanding debt?" Toks asked.

"I've got N283,440 and Ezzy has N147,780. We both knocked off N200k from our last debt," Soma said, excited.

"I'm glad to hear it and I'll drink to that," Toks said, pouring himself a drink.

"Make it two, I deserve a pat on the back for my good behavior." Ezzy grinned.

"Okay, any mortgage payments?"

"Check. Babe, how much are we paying a month?" Soma asked.

“Too much,” Ezzy scowled as he wrote the number down. “N187,400 with 48 months to go.”

“Credit card debt? Student loans.”

“None,” Soma said. “So what happens next?”

“Subtract your total liabilities from your total assets.”

“Ewoooo! What happens if the answer is negative?” Soma asked

“Then it means you simply haven't earned or invested enough money yet to overcome the weight of the debt.”

“Shiiiiiit!” Soma swore as her fingers scribbled furiously over the paper.

“Don't worry babe, it'll come,” Ezzy said, wrapping his arms around her.

“After all this time, I thought we were making progress…” Soma sniffed, cradling her face in her hands.

“We are, babe, it's not as bad as it used to be,” Ezzy comforted her.

“Then why do I feel so…”

“Damn…” Ezzy cursed.

“Happyyyyyy! Fooled ya!”Soma said, screaming. “Woohooo! Our net-worth isn't negative! Praise God.” Soma danced around the room.

“Oh Toks, thank you,” she gushed. “Thank you. You don't know how grateful I am. God bless you.”

“We done did it,” Ezzy said, with tears in his eyes. “We done did it.

TOTAL MONEY WORKOUT

1. To build your network, what problem should people have that's urgent and important to them for your name to be the solution?
2. On a scale of 1 to 100, rate your networking skills.
3. What can you do to improve your networking skills?

   How can the value you provide increase the clients value?

CHAPTER 12

CREATE THE FLOW THAT OTHERS FOLLOW

Secret 12: "Use leverage to buy you time and earn you money."

"You guys don't know how proud I am of you. We should definitely drink to this." Toks said, refilling their glasses.

"My work with you guys is almost over."

"Noooooo. Toks don't say that oh, we've only just gotten started," Soma said.

"So let's call this the end of the beginning."

"Man, if that's the case, then it's time to make it rain," Ezzy said.

"Then you better have a bucket," Toks replied.

"Huh? Dude, you lost me," Ezzy said.

"Here's what I mean, bro. We all want to make it rain, but we don't know how or when it's gonna rain; so it's as effective as waiting on a miracle. You dig?"

"Making sense so far," Soma responded as she scribbled into her notebook:

Rain = Expecting money to come by a miracle.

"Now, when it finally does rain, maybe we get some unexpected windfall, we just bask around, lounging, splashing in puddles and getting soaked; until the rain stops and then we realize too late that when it rains, everyone gets wet, but the person that takes water home, must have a bucket."

"Shiiiiittt. Dude, how the hell do you come up with these analogies? Guy, no time to waste time, abeg lay hands on me," Ezzy said, placing Toks' hand on his head.

"Na so. Let's get back to it. So in my opinion, making it rain is as good as expecting a miracle, and when it does come, we don't have a bucket to carry our blessings home. So guys, where's your bucket?"

"Omo, na to go market be dat."

"Unfortunately, that's the category most people fall into – waiting for rain to fall. They get a few sprinkles and showers here and there, but they're too busy getting wet that they don't get a bucket to save the water for when they're high and dry."

"Sounds a lot like how we used to be," Soma said.

"Still using water as an analogy, while others are staring into space, waiting for rain, a few are a lot wiser and have realized that instead of looking up for water, they could track the ground and follow the flow of water; and then, they discover rivers."

"*Follow the flow*, I like that" Soma said, scribbling.

"Yeah, but that's what a lot of people do until they discover there's a huge crowd at the river, with people kicking and screaming, all with their own buckets, each trying to get some water to take back home."

"Sounds rowdy," Soma said.

"Absolutely Soma, so while waiting for rain is the same as waiting for a miracle; going to the river is the same as fetching water you have to hustle for."

"That's deep," Ezzy said.

"I agree," Soma said, scribbling into her notebook.

"Rivers = Money you have to hustle for."

"I've seen a lot of entrepreneurs follow the flow only to realize that market is tapped out and saturated. They follow the flow into pure water business and get drowned, they follow the flow into MMM and their money misses magically, they follow the flow into what everyone seems to be doing and ultimately get trapped."

"So if you can't make it rain or follow the flow, na to build borehole be dat," Ezzy said.

"Exactly!"

"Huh?"

"You know you say the deepest things when you're not thinking," Toks said, patting Ezzy on the back.

"Yeah, I'm deep like that. But wait oh, what did I say?"

"You said if we can't make it rain or follow the flow, then build a borehole, or as I'd have preferred to say, a well."

"Nice. So we've got rain, rivers or wells," Soma said. "Why's a well different?"

"Simple. Let me put it this way. Rain hopes something's gonna flow, rivers follow the flow, but the well creates the flow that others follow."

"Baddo! Dude, we can still go on tour and get your rap career started. I'll be your hype man."

"Thanks man, but I'll pass."

"Toks, if I get you right, what you're saying is that the well is a system that already works for you."

"Absolutely, Soma! And like anyone who's dug a well knows, it's pretty messy and takes a lot of work to drill down and find water. But you truly can't be wealthy unless you own or have invested in a product or service that can make money for you, especially while you sleep."

"My money does the opposite. Keeps me awake at night," Ezzy scoffed.

"Not for long, bro, not for long. You need to realize that the only currency we have as a means of value exchange is time; and how we leverage it will determine how wealthy we become."

"Makes sense," Ezzy agreed.

"Like I've said so many times, the fundamental difference between the rich and poor is how they think, but also, how they use leverage. They either leverage their time or the time of others, or their money or other people's money. They are either leveraging other people's money or other people's time. So that's either OPM or OPT."

"You down with OPP?" Ezzy chanted.

"Yeah, you know me!" Soma chorused.

"You guys are just big kids," Toks said, shaking his head.

"--and proud of it," Soma said as she kissed her husband on the cheek.

"So, like I said before, time is the currency of life. Whatever we want to get from life, we must be willing to exchange time for it."

"Yup, if I wanna get that paper from my boss, I've gotta trade my 30 days to get it," Ezzy said.

"Let's calculate the value of your time, then. I wanna figure out how much your time is worth," Toks said.

"How are you gonna do that?" Ezzy asked curiously.

"Simple. Just tell me what your salary is," Toks said.

"I'm too embarrassed to even say, bro," Ezzy said, shaking his head.

"Fear fear! Toks, I'm game, I earn N276k after deductions," Soma said.

"Okay Soma, N276k," Toks said, scribbling into a paper.

"How many days do you work in a month?"

"I have to go to the office sometimes on weekdays, so let me say 22 days."

"Awesome. That means your daily rate is about N12,545."

"Blood of Jesus."

"It gets better," Toks grinned. "How many hours do you work a day?"

"I resume at 8am and can't leave after my Branch Manager, which is usually, say, 7pm. So let's say 11 hours."

"Okay, but let's include traffic to and from work."

"I'd say, let's add 3 hours in all."

"Okay, that's 14 hours," Toks scribbled. "That comes to N896 per hour."

"Holy Ghoooooosssstttt…" Soma screamed.

"Fire!" Ezzy responded, laughing.

"That's the value your organization places on your time per hour," Toks smiled.

"They're mad," retorted Soma.

"My friend, take this N1k and will you keep kwayet?!" Ezzy joked. "And yes, you can keep the change, bae."

"Taaah diabut bring the money first," Soma retorted.

"So now you can see what you're presently worth--" Toks said.

"No way oh. I'm worth more than that."

"So prove it. As you can see, earning N896 an hour isn't much, especially when you have to trade your time for it. That's why leverage is incredibly important. So if you had three staff that you were paying, say N100 an hour to sell or deliver on your business needs, you would be leveraging other people's time to get your desired results."

"I get it."

"Soma, how many staff work for your organization? It's a bank yeah?"

"Yeah. We have about three thousand people."

"So do you think the MD has 24 hours in a day to work with?"

"Technically yes, but since it's a trick question, I'm going to say no."

"You're absolutely right. Like you said, he technically has 24 hours that are limited to him, but has leveraged averagely 14 hours of 3000 staff per day. Leveraging other people's time is incredibly powerful, especially when you're a limited resource."

"You can say that again," Ezzy said.

"But Toks, what do you do if you don't have money to leverage anyone's time," Soma asked.

"You'll keep being limited and stand still."

"That's just cold."

"Truth hurts dear. Back in uni, we were taught in Economics class that the formula for income was rate multiplied by time (income = rate x time), remember that?"

"Yeah, vaguely, but yeah."

"In our quest for wealth, most people either focus on increasing their rates – how much they earn per hour – or by increasing their time; so people work two jobs to get more income. But that's a surefire recipe for disaster. Rich thinking people recognize that formula's not enough."

"So what's their formula?" Soma asked.

"It's rate multiplied by time multiplied by leverage, where leverage can either be people, money, knowledge or skills."

"Gotcha."

"Listen guys, you need to understand that one of the fundamental differences between the rich and poor is what they value."

"Yeah, money, right?"

"Not quite, but close enough. What they value more is their currency."

"Forex for the rich and Naira for the poor, abi?" Ezzy said grimly.

"Nah. Let me put it this way. The currency of the rich is time and the currency of the poor is money."

"Tweetable!" Soma said, scribbling into her notepad.

"The currency of the rich is time and the currency of the poor is money."

"That's deep."

"The poor person thinks having some money will make a difference, but the rich person thinks about how he can buy more time because he realizes that time is a more scarce resource than money; and how he leverages his time can earn him more money."

"Makes sense."

"Let's put it this way. Two people have to get from Lagos to Abuja in a day. One decides to take a bus and the other decides to fly."

"Omo, you have to cut your coat according to your material," Ezzy said.

"Understandably so. But let's go a little deeper. So the guy that decided to take a bus, sees that the standard fare by road in an air conditioned bus is say, N7k and will take about 12 hours, making only one stop to get to Abuja. But just as he's about to pay, he sees another bus that is just as air conditioned as the first, but is N6k, has two stops to make and the trip will take 15 hours. Which do you think he's going to take?"

"Definitely the cheaper one," Ezzy said.

"I'm so guilty. I did it on our last trip to Dubai. I picked the option of paying the cheaper price, with a six-hour layover, but with a longer trip instead of flying direct."

"But Toks, aren't we being prudent?"

"Depends on what you consider as being more valuable. Time or money? Sure I understand that there are certain situations that require you to cut your coat according to your cloth, but you've gotta ask yourself if you're just being a cheap skate *frugalista.*"

"Damn. Shots fired," Ezzy said, ducking for cover.

"You have to look at your patterns because they are predictive of your behavior."

"Sounds deep, bro, but I don't get it. I'm trying to figure it out."

"Your patterns are a signpost to where you're going. To know where you're going, you have to look at where you're coming from. You know when we go out to eat, we always decide what to eat based on the price. The items are on the left side of the menu, and the price is on the right side of the menu."

"Guilty as charged, Toks. I do that all the time. I no dey look the food at all, na the price I dey take style eye," Soma said.

"We're all guilty of that, dear. But check out what you said a moment ago, *I do that all the time*. So you've been programmed and conditioned to shop on the right side of the menu, and not just for food alone, I bet?"

"Yes oh. I do it for clothes, electronics, everything."

"That's because how you do one thing is how you do everything. So your patterns will predict that every time you have to make a purchasing decision, you will always value price over anything else."

"See my life."

"But here's the balance. I'm not asking you to go on a splurge fest and fulfill your base desires. If you do, you're taking a one-way ticket to being broke in no time. This is what I want you to do. Next time you're faced with making a decision that programs you to shop on the right side of the menu, ask yourself a simple question--"

"*What would Jesus*--Ouch!" Ezzy yelled as Soma pinched his thigh.

"Thanks, Soma," Toks said, shaking his head before continuing. "As I was saying, ask yourself, *will this purchase give me leverage or put me at a disadvantage?*"

"True word."

“So realize that getting wealthy isn't about having more money, it's about having more options.”

“Tweetable!” Soma said, scribbling.

“Getting wealthy isn't about having more money, it's about having more options.”

“But Toks, you know we work 9 to 5 jobs.”

“More like 9 to 9,” Ezzy scoffed.

“Like he said, we work 9 to 9 jobs,” Soma corrected herself, “how do we increase our options?”

“So right now, you guys are trading time for money. It's an unsustainable process, because you're running out of time, and someday, diminishing returns will set in, and if you can't give time to your work, you'll lose money.”

“Sounds scary.”

“So instead of trading time for money, you could leverage your resources to buy you time and earn you money.”

“I'm gonna say it this time, that right there is a tweetable.” Ezzy picked up Soma's notepad and scribbled.

“Don't trade time for money, leverage your resources to buy you time and earn you money.”

“That's deep, bro, flipping deep.”

“You're welcome,” Toks said, sipping his drink. “For example, if you wanted to leverage OPK, or *Other People's Knowledge,* one option is to create an offer or product that you can sell and deliver without having to be there. That's leveraging your knowledge.”

“How do you mean?” Soma asked.

"How long have you been a banker?"

"Slightly over 6 years. But to be exact, I'd say 6 years, 10 months and 27 days to be exact, but who's counting?"

"Definitely not you," Toks grinned. "What department have you spent the most amount of time working in?"

"Marketing," Soma said, rolling her eyes. "I need a new challenge. I've spent over 5 years there. I've been pushing HR to send me to Treasury, but it's like the cabal of Madam P and Aunty Booki won't let somebody be great."

"So over the last 5 years, do you think you've learned a thing or two on how to close deals or turn prospects into customers?"

"Me ke? I'm a pro. I can school you to the game—" Soma paused as it hit her, "Oh shit!"

"You see it now…" Toks grinned.

"See what? See what? What can't I see?" Ezzy asked, frustrated.

"See my life," Soma moaned. "I should be hearing the theme song, *Aiye le oo* playing in the background."

"Abeg, make I no lost. What's going on?"

"Toks, there's that thing you told us once, let me check my notepad." Soma flipped through her notepad. "Okay, I've found it. *It's not what you don't have that limits you, it's what you have, but don't know how to use* and then you once said that the word POOR is an acronym for *Passing Over Opportunities Repeatedly.*"

"I'm lost ooo," Ezzy complained.

"Toks just helped me realize the opportunities I've been passing over."

“Okay…?” Ezzy was on edge.

“So, I've been a banker for 6 years and in marketing for 5 years--”

“Ehen, go on!”

“My bank has over 3000 staff and let's assume that each of the 23 banks has an average of 3000 staff, that's 69,000 people.”

“Okay, so what's the problem?”

“If she turned her marketing experience into a product, let's say an ebook or online course--” Toks interjected. “And since all bankers need marketing skills, she'd have a captive market of at least 60,000 people.”

“--and if I sold a N2000 ebook to let's say, 5000 people…I'd make N10 million.”

“Shiiit!” Ezzy swore.

“I've been sitting on a bicycle,” Soma said.

“Now most bankers or employees in your situation would be blaming the organization for their stagnation, not realizing that not leveraging the opportunities that come their way by virtue of being in the company is entirely their fault.”

“I was one of them. I've blamed my company for the long hours and the insane targets, instead of realizing that my job is an opportunity to create value for my future line of work.” Soma said, ruefully.

“That's a tweetable, right there,” Ezzy said, scribbling into Soma's notepad.

“*My job is an opportunity to create value for my future line of work.*”

“Absolutely. That's when you decide to leverage your employment.

“Listen guys, think of leverage like a plot of land. What you build on it determines what you get back; and it all depends on your vision. Someone might decide to build a bungalow on that plot of land and choose to live in it. He's going to be free from his landlord and that's sufficient leverage. Another person might decide to build, say, a five-bedroom duplex with a boys quarters and rent it out, he's going to leverage that land to earn him rent from one or maybe, two individuals, who maintain his property and investment. Another person might decide to build a block of six flats, which earn him rent leveraged from six people; it's still the same plot of land. A final person might decide to build a shopping complex with thirty spaces, put them up for rent and he earns rent from thirty people. That's how powerful leverage is.”

“Wow. I never saw it like that before,” Soma said.

“Me neither. I've gotten a crash course in acquiring real estate too,” Ezzy said.

“It is what it is; and speaking about crash courses, I believe I've shared everything I understand and have experienced about making, managing and mastering money, over the last couple of months with you guys. I have nothing left to give.”

“Noooooo!” Soma refused “This can't be over. We've only just gotten started. We've only just gotten out of debt. What if we go back?”

“Then I'll kick both your asses,” Toks grinned. “Nah listen, guys, you'll be fine. Now your job is to pay it forward and leverage everything I've shared with you over these couple of weeks to grow your wealth. Test it, prove it and perhaps you can even come up with several other strategies to make mine obsolete.”

“That would be the day,” Ezzy scoffed, rolling his eyes.

“Stranger things have happened, bro.”

“Wow, Toks, I don't know what to say,” Soma said, her lips quivering. “I'm not going to cry. I'm not going to cry,” she muttered to herself, blinking back the tears welling up in her eyes.

"Me sef, for the first time, I'm speechless."

"That's definitely a first," Toks mocked Ezzy.

"Seriously man, I don't know how to thank you".

"You being speechless is more than enough thanks," Toks said slapping his friend on the back.

"I don't even know what to say. You've done so much for us. If it wasn't for you, we would've drowned in our financial failures" Soma said, her tears falling freely down her cheeks.

"So don't say anything," Toks said, hugging her. "Sometimes, God allows us fail so that those failures can inspire us and others to succeed."

"I know what you're thinking," Ezzy said, a mischievous smile creeping up his face.

"Tweetable!"

THE END.

TOTAL MONEY WORKOUT

1. Using either your salary or monthly income, calculate your hourly rate.
2. What patterns have you noticed that drive your financial decisions?
3. What could you do to stop trading time for money?
4. What opportunities have you been passing over?
5. What could you do to leverage - time, money, knowledge?

NOW THAT YOU HAVE READ THIS BOOK...

Let me guess?

You're waiting for some long, elaborate speech?

Nah, I'm done talking.

Now it's your turn to get moving.

Well, what are you waiting for?

Get to it.

GET IN TOUCH WITH STEVE...

Would you like to invite Steve Harris to speak at your organization or meeting?

Of course you do.

Call +234 809 658 1956 or +234 (01) 291 1718

Email: mail@iamsteveharris.com

Online: www.iamsteveharris.com

Social Media: @iamsteveharris (Instagram & Twitter)

Sign up for Steve Harris free email newsletter at:

www.iamsteveharris.com

To purchase bulk copies of this book at a discount for your friends or organization, please contact The Steve Harris Company at info@iamsteveharris.com